WALKING
with Glenn Berkenkamp

35 Wellness Walks to Expand Awareness,
Increase Vitality, and Reduce Stress

GLENN BERKENKAMP

North Atlantic Books
Berkeley, California

Published by   Cover art © gettyimages.com/ArdeaA
North Atlantic Books   Cover design by Jess Morphew
Berkeley, California   Book design by Happenstance Type-O-Rama

Printed in the United States of America

Walking with Glenn Berkenkamp: 35 Wellness Walks to Expand Awareness, Increase Vitality, and Reduce Stress is sponsored and published by the Society for the Study of Native Arts and Sciences (dba North Atlantic Books), an educational nonprofit based in Berkeley, California, that collaborates with partners to develop cross-cultural perspectives, nurture holistic views of art, science, the humanities, and healing, and seed personal and global transformation by publishing work on the relationship of body, spirit, and nature.

North Atlantic Books' publications are available through most bookstores. For further information, visit our website at www.northatlanticbooks.com or call 800-733-3000.

Library of Congress Cataloging-in-Publication Data

1 2 3 4 5 6 7 8 9 KPC 25 24 23 22 21 20

This book includes recycled material and material from well-managed forests. North Atlantic Books is committed to the protection of our environment. We print on recycled paper whenever possible and partner with printers who strive to use environmentally responsible practices.

MEDICAL DISCLAIMER: The following information is intended for general information purposes only. Individuals should always see their health care provider before administering any suggestions made in this book. Any application of the material set forth in the following pages is at the reader's discretion and is his or her sole responsibility.

Dedicated to walking.

And the stillness, feeling, seeing,

and understanding it can reveal.

And to Jack the cat.

For the gentleness he instilled in this project.

Walking: Advancing or traveling on foot at a moderate speed or pace by moving the feet alternately so that there is always one foot on the ground in bipedal locomotion.

Awareness: Knowledge that something exists, or understanding of a situation or subject at the present time based on information or experience.

Vitality: The capacity to live, grow, or develop.

Stress: A state of mental or emotional strain or tension resulting from adverse or very demanding circumstances.

Fun: Enjoyment, amusement, or lighthearted pleasure.

Contents

Preface   xi

Introduction   1

1   Why Should We Walk?   3

2   How Do *You* Walk?   7

3   The Evolution of My Walk   15

4   Some of My Favorite Walks   31

5   Before You Walk   39

6   The Walks   49

    WALK 1   Heel to Toe and Toe to Heel Balance Walks   53

    WALK 2   Turning and Tilting Your Head Balance Walk   61

    WALK 3   Walking Awake through Your Living Space   65

    WALK 4   Barefoot Grounding Walk   70

    WALK 5   Rain Walk   74

    WALK 6   Water Walk   78

    WALK 7   Inner Smile Walk   82

    WALK 8   Outer Smile Walk   85

WALK 9   Listening Walk   89

WALK 10   Making the World (or at Least Your
          Neighborhood) a Cleaner Place Walk   95

WALK 11   Walking Meditation (There and Back Style)   99

WALK 12   Walking Meditation (Circle Style)   104

WALK 13   Walking Meditation (Walking the Labyrinth)   108

WALK 14   Destination-Manifestation Walk   112

WALK 15   Earth Below, Heavens Above Walk   116

WALK 16   Full Moon Walk   120

WALK 17   Mindfully Walking Your Dog Walk   124

WALK 18   Forgiving Others Walk   129

WALK 19   Forgiving Yourself Walk   133

WALK 20   Dedication Walk   137

WALK 21   Prayer Walk   140

WALK 22   Affirmation Walk   145

WALK 23   Gratitude Walk   151

WALK 24   Seeing Walk   158

WALK 25   Centering Walk
          (a.k.a. Walking from Your Center)   165

WALK 26   Crowd Walking   172

WALK 27   Slow-Fast Walk   178

WALK 28   Slow Motion Walk   186

WALK 29   Soft Gaze Walk   191

WALK 30   Backward Walk   195

WALK 31   Grieving Walk   200

WALK 32   Working and Walking Things Out Walk   205

WALK 33   Head, Heart, Hara Walk   211

WALK 34   Seeing from Different Parts of Your Body Walk 217

WALK 35   Childlike Wonder Walk   224

Conclusion   229

"Which Walks to Do When" Guide   231

Affirmations and Intentions for Walking   241

Acknowledgments   247

About the Author   249

Preface

MY PARENTS WERE WALKERS. My mother still is. When I set out to write this book, I asked her what she receives from her walks. She shared that her daily walks not only energize her when she feels tired, but also provide her time to be more reflective and inwardly directed, even while taking in the world around her.

In my youth, we went for "after-dinner walks," usually around the suburban block where we lived in northern New Jersey. My father, an avid photographer who taught me by example to notice and appreciate the world in all its many shapes, colors, and forms, would also take his own long walks, often accompanied by our family dog. He would walk during his lunch breaks at work as well, sometimes with co-workers and sometimes alone.

My brother has always loved to explore areas on foot as well, and to this day he will do so while vacationing, getting a good feel for the environment and its people.

So walking, or "going for walks," is indeed something that I have inherited. And I consider it among the greatest of inheritances from my youth.

Over the years, my walks, and life, have deepened, ultimately leading to the writing and sharing of this book. May its walks and insights serve you well.

Introduction

I'VE TAKEN CASUAL WALKS, along with exercise-related walks and what I'll call "guided wellness walks," with hundreds of people throughout the years. When I lived in Los Angeles, I watched as the dog walker industry came to be.

I was a people walker. It wasn't an official title, as there was no such thing as "people walkers" in 1990s Los Angeles, but it was something I greatly enjoyed, whether with friends, family, or clients.

Once, at a party, I overheard a guest tell another guest that they "liked walking with Glenn Berkenkamp." It was an interesting sentence to hear. Many years later, while driving through Mill Valley, California, one of my favorite areas to walk in and explore, the idea of this book presented itself, along with its title: *Walking with Glenn Berkenkamp.*

I chose to keep this title because the title is not so much about a friend or friends, or even a past client, who may have enjoyed or benefited from our walks, but more the fact that wherever *I* walk, and whomever I may be walking with, I am always walking with me, Glenn Berkenkamp.

And so it is with you. As great an awareness outside of yourself, and within yourself, that you may cultivate, and however much you may change, grow, and evolve, you are still, and will always be while in this embodiment, you.

So as you partake in the walks presented in this book, you will walk with me, and in doing so, you will walk with you. In a most profound, interconnected, "all-is-one" manner, we are together, and we are also individuals. And the joy, beauty, and magic of it all is here.

In the pages to come, you will be asked to think about your physical walk, and your walk through life, and you will learn about my walk, along with some of my favorite walks taken.

You will be introduced to thirty-five wellness walks, along with an easy-to-use reference guide, "Which Walks to Do When," which can assist you in selecting the walk, or walks, best suited for you based on your current physical, mental, emotional, or spiritual needs.

You will discover that many of the walks are not only beneficial to you as an individual but also beneficial and fun to do with others, including walking groups and children.

From balance-building/balance-revealing walks to gratitude and forgiveness walks, to seeing and listening walks, to meditation and centering walks and many others—they are all very diverse. I encourage you to engage with each of them, and in doing so, allow yourself to awaken to the world, both within and around you, in new and exciting ways.

1

Why Should We Walk?

Walking is the best medicine.

—HIPPOCRATES

WHEN YOU LOOK AT a pencil, what does it reveal? Does it say anything? Other than the brand and number grade it has marked on it? No. But you know very well what it can do for you, what it can help you draw, or figure out, or erase. Sometimes just holding a pencil or pen between our fingers can make us more receptive to useful thoughts and inspired ideas that moments earlier did not exist for us. For me, it's as if I'm holding a receiver or antenna in my hand.

And so it is with walking. Yes, there's exercise. And exercise is of tremendous importance and value, especially in a society that has grown increasingly sedentary. But this book is about another form of value— more along the lines of stillness within movement, sensing and seeing, feeling, healing, and discovery—and of becoming free, or freer, and more connected in the process.

How do you become free *and* more connected while walking? By walking, and being truly present and mindful while doing so. And as you grow more present, expanding your awareness via certain types of walks and mental prompts, you will discover, often with the feedback of your body and a clearer mental state, how you are not free.

To use a computer term, I've found that walking, especially walking in nature, "reboots" human beings. I've witnessed the settling and clarity that arrive within people, making them more receptive and opening them to perspectives, insights, possibilities, and potentials not realized before. Coincidentally, I found this to be the perfect state to then introduce specific guided wellness walks that will serve them best.

Albert Einstein described his daily walks as "sacred," and, along with his famed naps, felt his daily walks greatly contributed to his process of trying to solve the larger questions of existence.

Hippocrates, the father of modern medicine, said that walking is the best medicine. Science continues to show us just how life-enhancing this "medicine" is.

"Going for a walk" requires absolutely no skills, other than the ability to walk, and can be done at any time, day or night, free of charge. And walking brings benefits just by the very action itself.

So before we go deeper, and we will go deeper, much deeper, it is important to establish here that the decision to go for a walk, to get outside, to move, is one of the best decisions you can make. Allowing yourself this time for you speaks to your ability and desire to tend to your own well-being. This is a tremendous gift to yourself, and therefore, a gift to us all. For when you're at your best, you can be your best for others. And there are more gifts to come.

It is my desire to introduce you to an ever-deepening, enjoyable exploration of one of the most basic human acts, one often not thought of, reflected upon, nor even considered of much value—other than for exercise or to transport us from point A to point B. At a time when electronic screens dominate our attention, I am here to tell you that a whole world exists between these two points. And seeing that world, and *how* you see it, experience it, and "play" within it, will tell you much about yourself and the town, city, country, and universe through which you move.

Walking with Limitations

Many of you reading this may be in pain of one kind or another. Physical pain can very well be a deterrent to walking; emotional pain can be as well. Knowing this, you must remain aware and pace yourself accordingly (but not purely based on the past, and what may or may not have occurred, but based on the present). Walking, and the deeper practices you may integrate and connect with while doing so (more on this later), can often have profound and lasting healing effects on the body.

This book may also reach someone who is unable to physically walk, someone using a wheelchair, walker, or other mobility device. For those in this situation, I wish to say that a great percentage of what is being shared here will still apply. It will help you connect deeper into yourself and your surroundings, and may even lead to a deeper, more nuanced relationship between you and those who are assisting you. Look for this to occur. Allow it to occur.

Autopilot versus Pilot

Mindful (or conscious) walking is one of the greatest tools we have to get ourselves off autopilot—the internal program that has been running our mind and body for years, often filled with self-defeating patterns, unconscious actions and reactions, and blind spots surrounding aspects of our life. It will help us become the *pilot* ... or at least deeply aware of how we fly, or in this case, how we walk ... or even simpler, how we can just *be*.

From what you learn in this book, you will cultivate the ability to better understand and discover how you move, think, feel, sense, and operate in your body; and with this comes a greater state of awareness and presence. As this begins to unfold and deepen, you will find yourself with a clearer understanding of who you are in relationship to your body and the manifest world outside of you. You will learn how to more deeply reside in your being; and blind spots will be revealed, reduced, and even eliminated.

In this moment, I would like to point out that stationary meditation, whether seated or lying, is a highly beneficial awareness-growing practice to engage in—one that yields profound benefits. But we want to work with walking. And seeing. We want to take meditation beyond the mat or chair and engage our surroundings in a very tactile way. And in doing so, you will take meditation into the world.

When you become the *pilot,* meaning when you are present and mindfully connected in a moment-to-moment way to your body, understanding your actions and where and why they originate, and initiate your actions and movements from this conscious place, you experience life in new, and what often may appear to be miraculous, ways. You hear more, *both externally and internally,* you see more, *both externally and internally,* and you feel more, *both externally and internally.* In short, you become the very embodiment of wholeness.

You are reset and at a clean starting point. From this place, you are at your most potent. Your body, mind, and spirit are aligned. Walking can be that powerful. Walking *is* that powerful.

2

How Do *You* Walk?

WE EACH HAVE A relationship to the word and the activity of walking. What is walking to you? A pleasure? A chore? A pain? A nonthought? An afterthought? An escape? A blessing? A teacher? Is it pure exercise, when you think about it at all, or is it something that you actively and consciously participate in? And by consciously, I am referring to: Are you there? Are you truly in the body? Are you present to yourself and your surroundings? Or are you tuned-out, distracted, on autopilot?

Take a moment to reflect on these questions and then answer the original question: "What is walking to you?"

Knowing and understanding what walking is to you at this point is important, especially because your relationship to walking may very well soon change.

In this chapter, take some time to think about the questions being asked, which you may not have considered before. Take equal time to reflect on your answers.

Before engaging in the questions, you may even wish to take a short walk, perhaps around your own living space.

I recommend that you write the questions down on a piece of paper or on another physical object that you can refer to later. I encourage you to ask these same questions of your family, friends, walking group, or anyone else you like to walk with. You may also wish to ask a positive, supportive friend or family member to give feedback that will help you answer some of the questions.

NOTE The questions in this section are not meant to overload you or put you too much "in your head." They are placed here as a way for you to grow more connected in the understanding of your body and your overall being and awareness.

Describe in your own words:

- What is your walk like? What does it feel like? What does it look like?

- Is your walk smooth, or does your movement feel ratchety and clunky?

- Does it feel as if your body operates and moves as one fluid organism, or more like an assemblage of separate parts that do not move in concert or communicate well with each other? (The latter might happen when the different parts of your body receive different signals due to stress, genetics, injury, or even intentional walking patterns you've developed; see more about this in chapter 3, "The Evolution of My Walk.")

- Do your arms move when you walk, or do they stay stationary at the sides of your torso?

- Do your shoulders move when you walk? Do they "ride high," meaning they tend to stay up near your ears? Are they slumped or rounded forward?

- Is your spine long when walking? Do you feel a sense of freedom in your spine when you walk?

- Are your hands relaxed when you walk?

- What is your breathing like when you walk?

- Do your heels or the balls of your feet strike the ground first when walking?

- Can you feel the workings of your hips and pelvis?

- Are your arms and legs moving contralaterally? When your left leg goes forward is your right arm going forward as well? This is how you are designed to move.

- When walking barefoot, are you aware of each area of your foot as you walk?

- Do you have a natural stride that feels most comfortable to you? If so, can you identify that stride?

- Does your head feel free to move in all directions when you walk?

- Do you feel connected to the ground? This may seem like an odd question, but it's important. How we perceive our relationship to the ground is very revealing, as it helps us to see "holding patterns"—unnecessary muscular tension—throughout the body and how they affect our center of gravity and our connection to the ground.

- Do you feel self-conscious? If so, can you identify why?

- In general, do you notice your surroundings when you walk? This is not limited to outdoors or when "going for walks" but refers to your day in general.

EXERCISE

Close your eyes and see yourself walking. Try to tune in and relive your experiences of places where you walked today or on an average day. Try to really *see* yourself walking through your day, as if you're watching a replay of a movie.

Once you can do this, then try to *see* and *feel* yourself walking through your day. Can you connect the visualization with a physical feeling? See and feel how you encountered and moved through various moments throughout your day.

Were there moments when you felt lighter? Heavier? Happier? Clearer? What was your breathing like?

Can you identify highs and lows from your day and how they affected your walk, your breath, and your energy in general? And do you view these as common occurrences?

Now, can you *hear* yourself move through your day? Are you loud? Quiet? Do you like to be noticed, perhaps the center of attention? Do you wish not to be seen? Are there times when you are a little of each?

Which part or parts of your day were the easiest to see or recall? Were there gaps in your day that you just passed over or either couldn't see or didn't want to see, feel, or hear in replay?

Which part or parts of your day were the easiest to feel?

Which part or parts of your day were the easiest to hear?

In general, when someone passes you, what kind of person are they passing? Will they feel they are passing a happy person? A sad person? An angry person? An open person? A tired person? A closed-off person? A stressed person? A heart-centered person?

Granted, we as humans are dynamic organisms who are often changing from moment to moment, so being happy, open, and heart-centered is not always an everyday, every moment occurrence. There will certainly be times when we are walking to unwind, find peace, de-stress, or regroup. In those moments, a passerby may not be encountering an outwardly happy being. But the question for you is more about your deeper nature, where you're currently at, and whether you view—or can view—yourself as a happy person, a heart-centered person, a person who meets life in a positive manner. And if not now, can you see it in your near future?

I am sure that answering these questions has led you into thoughts and understandings about yourself and your walk that you may not have had before.

There is certainly an ideal walk one can reach for and read about in walking books, or in exercise physiology books, or even by studying the teachings of the Eastern masters who have come to understand ease of movement in the most beautiful, elegant, and effective ways. (We will discuss ease of movement more later, especially in chapters 3 and 6, but for now consider it a seed planted.) We are all unique, and what goes into that uniqueness is vast and, as stated above, often changing.

We can all strive to walk (and move through life) in the healthiest way for our body, including what is dictated by our structure, past and present injuries, emotional hurts and pains, mental traumas, etc.

I find that a positive attitude and the ability and desire to let go, forgive ourselves and others, and embrace that often-challenging, but oh-so-important, "self-love" can really help bring ease and inner and outer radiance to our walk throughout life. So you may never be a smooth, balanced, and flowing walker, but you will grow more and more aware of your habits, patterns, quirks, and the limitations of your walk. And in doing so, you will bring a great deal more comfort and even mobility into your life.

It is my belief that the walks and concepts outlined in this book will help lead you there.

Body Awareness

One tip that I will share, that speaks to much of what this book is about, is to become aware of the parts of your body—even if it's just one—that are working well. And by this I mean moving freely, without strain, tension, or injury. Find these areas and fully inhabit them. Even if it's just one wrist, play around in its freedom and ease of movement. Really enjoy it, marvel at it, and have gratitude for it. Then allow, starting with your mind's eye or imagination, this freedom and ease to ripple outward into other—and all—areas of your body. See how far your mind can take you.

I am hesitant to place this "mechanics of walking" list here as I do not want you to be overly focused on walking mechanics. But I feel I would be remiss to not at least present some basic guidelines featuring the physical mechanics of walking in a book where the focus is on walking.

Later in the book, you will find a different set of walking guidelines, including a Pre-Walk Check-In, that are more specific to the teachings and philosophies outlined in the book.

- Stand tall. Spine long. (But remain relaxed, not rigid.)
- Your head straight.
- Your chin parallel to the ground.
- Your shoulders relaxed. (Not riding up toward your ears.)
- Your neck aligned with your shoulders, not forward. (For many of you, this may be uncomfortable and cause pain. If that's the case for you, do not try to force your neck and head back; rather, become aware of it and adjust as you can over a period of time.)
- Your eyes looking forward.
- Some walking experts recommend that you draw (visualize) a straight line from your ear down to your shoulder, to your hip, knee, and ankle.
- Your hands relaxed.
- Your arms slightly bent at the elbows. (This is suggested mainly for race/speed walking.)
- Allow shoulders to move naturally.
- When in walking motion, your heel will hit the ground first, then roll gently toward the front of your foot and your toes. You will then push off your toes (big toe actually) as you propel yourself forward.

Practicing some of these principles indoors can be very helpful.

Remember, *it's the whole of you—the entirety of you—that walks.* Not parts of you. And if you'd like, you can extend this beyond the physical and say it is the mind, body, and spirit that walk.

3

The Evolution of My Walk

FROM YOUR RELATIONSHIP TO walking, to mine.

We all have a path that we travel through life. You could say it's our story. And for the most part, we are *walking* that path through its many chapters.

I will share a bit about my path, most specifically as it relates to my walk. In doing so, my hope is that it will bring you deeper understanding of your walk/path, and even your story.

First Steps

Do you remember your first steps? I don't recall mine, but being that my father was an avid photographer who recorded much of my brother's and my childhood, I was fortunate to have seen pictures and Super 8 movie footage of this momentous occasion. On the surface, it really did not look like anything extraordinary, other than a young boy determined to find his upright place in this world. But if we think about it, and become aware of all that must take place throughout the body to bring a human being from crawling, to standing, to then walking—the communication from the brain to various parts of the body, the muscular system, the nervous system, etc., the perfect timing and organizing required—it is no doubt mind-boggling and incredible. And it also is something that never stops: this complex process occurs with every movement—large or small, slow or fast—we make. And those of us fortunate enough to be able to walk are in a position to explore this chain of internal happenings in a way that can open us up to the magic (and understanding) of movement and the moment, and the lessons and blessings found within each.

From those first steps until now, I've been fortunate. My relationship to walking has never been hindered by serious injury, illness, or affliction—although as a bodybuilder I did challenge my body a great deal over the years and certainly felt my share of aches and pains.

In many ways, I hope that this book takes you back to the wonder and nuance of those first steps—and the many steps since—and also shows you that it's almost never too late to undo less-than-optimal habits that have been formed and imprinted over the years. And if you cannot fully undo them, you may at least understand them and create new, healthier ones.

Single-File in Elementary School

My first recollection of any kind of organized walking was walking and standing in line during the early years of my schooling. It was probably kindergarten and first grade where we had to be careful (and mindful) of the child directly in front of us, so as not to bump them or give them a "flat tire"—the front of our foot causing the back of their shoe to get pulled down and under their foot.

This was my, and I'm assuming many others', early introduction to pace (yours and another's), stride, timing, personal space/boundaries, and of course "rules." (As we know, most children have a great deal of energy, and trying to get twenty or more—or even two or more, for that matter—to move at the same pace and rhythm can prove challenging. *It can also be viewed as a great awareness exercise, when kids are shown how to do it mindfully, with as much attention as they can muster at such a young age.*)

I also recall running outdoors on the way to the designated playground area, only to be told to slow down and walk—and often to once again form a single-file line.

Looking back, it would have been beneficial (and really cool) to have had teachers who could have been able to help the kids get more out of this, to get us more in touch with the mechanics of our body, along with our mind and emotions … and even make slowing ourselves down *fun*. (Be sure to try the Slow Motion Walk on page 186. And when possible, share it with a child.)

As I reflect now on these early years of instilled or "forced" order, I can see how it did help prime me in the ways of becoming more aware of my own and another's pace, personal space, and unique rhythms. All these understandings have served me well when walking with others throughout the years. And I do know that my early schoolteachers did their very best. I am grateful for them and their desire to keep me and others safe. And I look forward to sharing many of these walks, including the Slow Motion Walk, in more and more schools.

Walking with My Family in My Youth

As I mentioned earlier, my family were walkers. After dinner, on weekends, etc. But I never *thought* about walking: there was never any focus on or awareness of how I walked or how to walk, beyond the physical act of just doing it. Being that I was of healthy body, I was on autopilot, like most everyone. The only time my mind would go to that place of heightened awareness would be on those rare occasions when I got a splinter in my foot, a bee sting on my foot, a cramp in my leg, or perhaps stubbed my toe and then was forced to see what now wasn't working, or was no longer "easy" to do, or how I had to perhaps favor another area of the foot—or the complete other leg.

Even during my sporting pursuits, whether it be in team sports or individual pursuits, I never thought about movement or what was happening within me. It was just "Run to there," "Walk to there," "Stand there," "Bend your knees when playing the field in baseball," etc. And perhaps there is no need to overload a developing child with information about walking and greater awareness around movement. But I can't help thinking that there are missed opportunities here, opportunities that could help us tune into who we are and ultimately how we live in these bodies that we may end up inhabiting for eighty-plus years. Along with this, we could also perhaps increase athletic performance and head off detrimental habits that lead to injury, unnecessary strain, and wear and tear.

So, this is what I did *not* think about or consider during our family walks or on other occasions.

But what I *did* take away from our walks as a young boy was all that we saw, noticed, and discovered.

I say discovered because that was often the case—so-and-so painted their house, so-and-so planted a garden, so-and-so's daffodils are blooming, the grass is growing, a fence was damaged, a new car was purchased, and so forth. So these walks imparted in me an appreciation of my surroundings, and the desire to see, note, and *feel*—I say feel because many of these visual cues or even scents triggered a specific feeling in me—changes as they occurred. Much of this was pointed out by my parents and my older brother.

So even though my body was on autopilot, my eyes and mind were engaged in a way that was very beneficial.

This foundation from youth has stayed with me and has of course been deepened as I engaged in mindfulness and awareness style walks, alone and with others, throughout these last thirty years. But for many years it was absent, as my focus became fully on my physical development.

Bodybuilding

From the age of twelve into my early twenties, I was focused on gaining muscle mass and understanding strength and muscular development in general. I was a bodybuilder, a physique judge—judging such competitions as Mr. USA—and I trained and advised many top amateur and professional bodybuilders.

Over those years my relationship to my ever-changing body, including how I carried and expressed it while walking, due partly to natural growth and development through adolescence, along with intense training and supplementation, brought my walk through interesting phases.

It was also during this time that I started to understand the body in greater detail. Or you could say, I started to explore it—at least the muscular system—in great detail. But since the task of a bodybuilder is to sculpt and concentrate on the individual muscles, even to the point of how they are paired together while training, which muscles to stimulate while the others are resting, etc., it was in a very compartmentalized way. So as much as one is striving for a well-proportioned, balanced, and symmetrical physique, one is still approaching it from the various *parts,* as opposed to understanding it as a *whole.* Of course, there is a nutritional and presentational (posing) element that does take into account feeding, supporting, and viewing the body as a whole, so it is not always viewed as fragments, but most often one is focusing on individual muscles—any of which may be lagging behind at any given time—and the muscular system in general.

I have a light bone structure, what is classified as an ectomorph, so adding muscle to my frame took a great deal of work, and in some ways it was forced upon my body since ectomorphs generally don't carry a lot of muscle mass. There were times when I would feel the weight in a delightful "look what I'm accomplishing" way—but there were other times when it felt as though the weight was literally weighing me down, making me slower, duller, less sharp in my movement.

There is a great deal of tension placed on the body. You rarely describe a bodybuilder, at least from a physical perspective, as being loose and relaxed, especially when walking. Muscles become "rock hard" (a compliment) and often overly contracted—and often so does the one wearing them. Having said this, I would be remiss not to mention that there are quite a few bodybuilders who remain extremely fluid and flexible (both mentally and physically).

My walk through this period took on various forms.

Two I recall well. I would flex my calves while walking by rising up and down on my toes to engage the calf muscles. This would give my calves extra stimulation, in hopes of even more growth, and accentuate and show off, while wearing shorts, a body part that I worked very hard to develop. This was never a pattern that grooved itself into my brain—I did not find myself walking this way without trying to do so—it was something I was aware of and doing consciously.

The second favoring or accentuation I would often do—also related to displaying muscle development, this time in the quadriceps—was to shake or kind of kick out my thighs when I walked. This would cause the muscles to move from side to side, which felt good, but I'm sure I also did it because it looked good, or at least I thought it did.

As with the rising up and down on my toes to exercise my calves, the shaking of the thigh muscles never became an ingrained pattern. This was good, since both ways of walking, done over an extended period of time, would most certainly cause imbalances and unnecessary stress throughout the body.

When your back (latissimus dorsi muscles, or your "lats") gets wider, it pushes your arms out—we've all seen the muscleman V-taper look—and shifts how you walk. So this became part of my walk as well. Interestingly, the gym where I did a great deal of my training had a saying: "You have to earn your wings," and this went right along with another saying they had: "You have to be big before you can walk big." Once you "earn your wings" (your developed lats) and can "walk big," you do so. And you do so simply because this is how your body is now put together—where emphasis is on this external accomplishment and you tune deeper and deeper into the nuances of these individual muscles, with the larger muscle groups dominating the walk.

My highest weight was around 230 pounds. At six-foot-three that is not very heavy for a bodybuilder, especially by today's standards where men who are five-foot-seven or less compete at or around that weight. But for me, especially as I reflect back on it now, it was a tremendous accomplishment.

I say "especially as I reflect back on it now" because at the time I was never satisfied with my body—and self-acceptance was cast aside for self-discipline.

Physical development also gives you a certain confidence and presence, and at times a definition of sorts of who you are. This adds to your walk. When you feel good about yourself, or feel you have obtained a level of strength and command over the body, you tend to enter a space in a way that is different from the version of you that may feel shy, weak, nervous, or in the case of many bodybuilders, previously unseen. You now fill space in an interesting manner.

Throughout my journey in bodybuilding, and later working with other athletes and nonathletes, I recognized the importance of the mind-muscle connection. It is something I would stress to all those I was training. It became increasingly clear that the more present one was, the more they were mentally tuned into the muscle throughout the entirety of the movement—including moments prior and after—the faster the gains would come. Visualization was also an important element.

Having lived and explored this firsthand through my training experiences, I was primed for further understanding of the mind-muscle (and overall mind-body) connection in the years to come.

One could say that my path, and my walk, was unfolding perfectly.

From Rock to Water

In his wonderful, poignant book, *From Rock to Water: A Healing Journey*, Nino Surdo dedicates a chapter to me. Nino mentions that I "taught him how to walk." He goes on to explain that I taught him how to slow down, see, and appreciate his surroundings—and in doing so, also appreciate himself, his path (as painful as it may have been at the time), and the role he played in this world. He learned that there was more. And he learned how to see it and experience it in a way that had a positive impact on his daily life and the lives of those around him.

After forcing and fighting his way through life, Nino went from rock to water—finding softness, flow, and ease—and by no means did he lessen his strength. Remember, water is strong enough to penetrate and shape rock.

Nino's path and my path have similarities. Namely, we were both bodybuilders who set out to find another form of strength—and a new relationship to our body and the world as well.

When I was twenty-three, after being deeply engrossed in body-building for ten-plus years, I made the decision that I was now going to work on my "insides" as much as I had worked on developing my outside. I had no idea what that would entail, but I knew it felt right to me, and it was. And so began my own journey inward, taking me from rock to water.

As you have come to realize, this book is about how walking reflects on our daily life—our habits, patterns, beliefs, psychological makeup, etc.—rather than being just something we physically do at leisure or for exercise. So as our thinking, along with our beliefs and interests, changes, our walk, and how we exist in our body, also tends to change. Nonetheless, as stated earlier, it is the whole of us, the "all of us" that walks. This includes our thoughts, beliefs, emotions, fears, dreams, desires, hurts, pains, elations, loves, and everything in between.

Take a moment now and think about how you walk when you're happy versus when you're sad, calm versus stressed, confident versus shy, confused versus clear. You understand what I am conveying here. You get it. You see it. You maybe even can feel it. But often, we are not aware of it. We are especially not aware of it when we settle into our "normal" everyday life that is, for many of us, one big blur of "doing" and very little "being." In other words, many of us are not really here. Not in the moment. Not present. Once again, we are on autopilot. And we usually only come off autopilot when we crash.

What did it mean for me to work on my insides? It meant taking a good look at myself (including "Who am I without these developed muscles?")—my fears, insecurities, habits and patterns, beliefs, as well as what made me tick, physically, mentally, and spiritually—both as an individual and in relation to the world. It meant really beginning the path of "Know thyself" that ultimately leads to self-mastery.

The first thing I began to do was observe my thoughts. (Why did I think a certain way? And where were these thoughts originating from?) Then my beliefs. (Why did I believe the things I believed?) I wanted to understand my operating system. And what was there that I was not consciously aware of?

When we slow down enough—mentally and physically—we afford ourselves the opportunity to get to know ourselves. This is what I was learning, along with the fact that slowing down and going inward can at times be a very uncomfortable process, as much of what is underneath is now brought to the surface.

Here's a funny story from when I first wanted to learn how to meditate. I purchased a cassette tape on meditation. What stuck out to me was the person's voice telling me at the very beginning of the tape that "you cannot learn how to meditate." I remember the frustration I felt when I heard this statement. Why did I buy (and why did they produce and promote) a tape on meditation if it could not be taught? It seemed so bizarre, especially since I could not sit still for much more than a minute, and needed all the help and insights I could get.

What I came to realize was that part of learning to meditate (and becoming more peaceful and present) was undoing—or unlearning—what was keeping me from presence and peace to begin with. Once this process began, sitting (and "being") became easier. Meditation tools such as working with my breath, focusing on the flame of a candle, and other tips proved very useful. But self-observation, even when (or especially when) moving fast, when off-center, angry, stressed, challenged, or confused, in a seeming sea of chaos, etc., was a huge step. How do I react in these moments? When do I tense up? Why do I tense up? How long do I hold the tension? Am I aware of where the tension takes hold in my body? Do I have a way to release it?

I learned a very important truth that has been taught by the wise ones for eons: change comes from observation. Of course we then have to do (or undo) something with this observation. But the very act of observing and realizing something for the first time sets off a cascade of change and greater understanding.

Who Did I Think I Was?

Prior to embarking on this inner chapter of my life, everything external took precedence for me: how I looked, what automobile I drove, what my girlfriend looked like (and, more importantly, what she looked like in society's eyes), what new objects and toys I could purchase to make me feel good—and fit in with our culture's overall version of success. I also viewed myself purely as a physical being, meaning that there was no thought of any aspect of me perhaps existing beyond the physical.

I'd like to state here that we are all walking our own path, and there is nothing wrong with this external-dominant view of yourself and the world, except for when your self-worth and well-being are tied to these external pursuits, and what often become conquests. One doesn't build a house on shifting sands. And for the most part, the external pleasures and manifestations we seek are very much like shifting sands. They provide no real long-term sense of well-being. I still love and appreciate fine automobiles, etc., but I seek to not tie my worth to what I do, or do not, own.

Finding Strength in Ease

I've found that ease of mind and ease of body often go hand in hand. Tight mind. Tight body. Rigid mind. Rigid body.

I did not go easily into ease. At times I still don't. I find that my default setting is to tighten up, dig in, and get it done. There is nothing inherently wrong with this—when it is called for. The challenge (and treat) is to understand when you are over-working, over-efforting, getting tense and constricted for no reason other than that's all you know.

If I could offer one broad piece of advice that I feel would lead to a deeper state of well-being for anyone reading this, it would be to familiarize yourself with the work of Moshé Feldenkrais.

Moshé Feldenkrais was an Israeli physicist, mechanical and electrical engineer, and judo expert. After a knee injury threatened to leave him unable to walk, he used his knowledge of physics, body mechanics, and neurology to develop exercises to help teach the body easier, more efficient ways to move. This became what is known as the Feldenkrais Method, and from there Awareness Through Movement (or simply, ATM) exercises and classes were formed.

Feldenkrais's discoveries about the body—most specifically, how the brain and the nervous system affect the muscles, and the Awareness Through Movement exercises that were born of these discoveries and explorations, along with the one-to-one Functional Integration® (FI) process he taught to practitioners—are nothing short of transformative … and for many, bordering on the miraculous.

I'd like to share a story about how Feldenkrais's teachings first came into my life. I was in my late twenties or early thirties, and I had been working on overall wellness with the aid of a qigong master. For those who are not familiar, *qi* (life force energy) *gong* (cultivation) is an ancient Chinese healing art comprising coordinated body-postures and movement, breathing, and meditation.

The work this master and I would do revolved around balancing the body's energy and increasing vitality.

One day, when I was walking in to see him, he said to me, "You barely use your left leg. It's literally sliding along getting a free ride from your right leg." I had no conscious connection to—or better described, no conscious feeling of—what he was noticing and describing to me. He then instructed me to walk toward him three or four times, each time giving me a prompt that would guide me into more presence and connection to my legs.

Finally, he said, "Let me show you something. Take off your sneakers." So I did. He said, "Turn them over." I did, and just looked at them, blindly, not noticing anything out of the ordinary. He asked, "Do the heels look the same?"

I then realized that my left heel was worn down to a far greater degree than my right heel.

My thoughts were immediately, Was one leg longer? One hip higher?

Or was it his answer, paraphrased here: "There is unnecessary muscular tension causing the natural chain of movement not to occur as designed to occur."

From this moment on, we set out to correct this. And we did so without any physical manipulation: no chiropractic, no orthopedic insert in my shoe, no deep massage, just awareness, and Feldenkrais-based exercises to release muscular (and mental) tension starting from the ankle and working our way up.

To make sure that I could actively track my progress, I purchased the same sneakers—Adidas Trail Runners—throughout the process. As for duration, I'm not sure exactly how long it took, but by the time I was wearing down my second new pair of Trail Runners, they wore out nearly identically on each heel and the rest of the sole.

I will not go in depth about the full process, but I will describe the first exercise he had me do, which seemed to unlock what needed to be unlocked for me and allowed everything else that followed to fall into place.

I'd like to note that techniques such as these cannot heal all physical ailments and limitations; but they may bring you a greater awareness and understanding of them, and certainly assist you on your healing journey.

The steps of the exercise are:

1. Lie down comfortably on your back on a couch, bed, or massage table with your heels extending slightly over the edge.

2. As best you can, relax your entire body.

3. In your mind's eye, envision either foot (it's your choice which foot to begin with) bending at the ankle and moving slowly and smoothly upward toward your chin, and then back downward.

4. Once you can see this occurring in your mind's eye, take a moment, then physically perform the same movement.

The trick—and instruction—is to perform this movement with as little tension, shakiness, or recruiting from other areas (for example, you're doing the ankle exercise but feeling tension or engagement in your jaw) as possible and to really "listen" with your inner listening to what is happening throughout your body.

Here's what I recall noticing: When I first attempted to perform what was on the surface a simple exercise, I could feel all the "clicks" or "ratcheting" in my ankles as I would raise and lower them. I could also feel tension (or unneeded recruiting/activation) through my chest, neck, and jaw. So it became clear that I was over-efforting and calling upon other muscles to perform this very simple task.

Each day for many weeks I would do this exercise, first seeing it in my mind's eye, and each time there would always be various degrees of ratcheting and tension found somewhere—although they were becoming greatly reduced—until one day when something odd, yet very revealing and important (and extremely cool) happened:

> When I was visualizing my left foot moving effortlessly up in my mind's eye, all of a sudden I realized that my foot *was indeed moving effortlessly up*—so effortlessly it was as if it was floating.

From that day on, I could relive this over and over, and go on to perform the exercise physically with the same ease and fluidity as I could perform it in my mind's eye. *Talk about a mind-body connection!* This was far deeper than anything I had experienced in my mind-muscle bodybuilding days.

I realized that if I could accomplish this in one part of the body, I could accomplish it in all parts of the body. When I told my teacher this, his response was: "Exactly."

This exercise allowed me to see that I did not know my body as well as I thought I did. It also drove home the point that less is indeed more. Again, excessive force (or effort) versus ease. And knowing when to call upon either.

From that day on, the overall task was to invite more and more ease into my body until it could once again do what it was designed to do without hidden tensions, etc., getting in the way.

To this day, twenty-some-odd years later, my shoes still wear down evenly. If you feel so inclined, I encourage you to flip your shoes over and check out the soles.

Affirmations

I've frequently talked about acting on autopilot, as in acting without conscious awareness. And how when we consciously connect to certain positive habits, they can eventually work on autopilot—becoming part of our "normal" way of thinking, feeling, and being. Affirmations, for example—especially positive affirmations—played a large role in my journey inward, helping me to better track and understand my thoughts, beliefs, and self-talk, and to begin to shift them in a way that would better serve myself and others.

If you think about it, each and every moment you are affirming something about yourself and the world. And for the most part, much of what you are affirming may be happening below your conscious awareness. You can think of positive affirmations as positive statements spoken to yourself.

In some circles, positive affirmations are looked down upon. This is often because of the ungrounded, overly positive person who may be espousing them. But what about "negative" affirmations? When presented with the statement that positive affirmations are ridiculous or "New Age" or whatever else, my reply has often been, "How about negative affirmations? What are your feelings about them?" This is often met with a perplexed look.

Very few of us are aware of the unconscious messaging that plays like a tape in our minds, and much of these tapes are self-defeating, world-defeating, tiring, and filled with untruths.

The idea of positive affirmations starts first with identifying the negative affirmations and seeing how your life would be if you made the switch from negative to positive—or harsh to kind, counterproductive to productive, selfish to serving, disempowering to empowering, faith-less to faith-filled, etc. Simply put, engaging in the process of affirmations does two things: helps you to become aware of your current tape, and helps you to create a new, more beneficial tape that can lead to profound changes in your life.

A positive affirmation may be as simple as "I approve of myself" to the more complex "The universe is perfect; everything I need flows to me."

There are many books on affirmations. The one that I am most familiar with, and found to be very helpful, is Louise Hay's *You Can Heal Your Life*. The above affirmations came from there.

Whether you engage in positive affirmations or not is your choice, but do watch your thoughts and self-talk, and give the Affirmation Walk (page 145) a try. If nothing else, I think you'll find it interesting.

I also think you'll find that we as humans often get proof of our thoughts and beliefs manifesting in our lives. So it's up to us to pay attention and see how much we are drawn into—and often are creating or co-creating—situations based on our thoughts and beliefs.

Breath

One final ingredient that has really taken me deeper into wellness and how I could navigate the world, both inner and outer, and the many situations that came my way, is breath.

Conscious breathing truly is the key that unlocks many of the closed doors and constricted pathways within us. It is a tool, free of charge and always available, that can help us through many situations. We'll go much deeper into breath in chapter 6, but for now I'll leave you with some of the most common, and wonderful, benefits of conscious breathing.

Proper breathing improves circulation, reduces stress, calms your nervous system, increases energy—and the supply of nutrients and oxygen throughout your body—massages and stimulates your organs, aids in digestion, clears your system of toxins and carbon dioxide waste, and eases pressure on your heart. And again, all this, and more, for free.

Now

As of writing this, I am quite happy with my walk. This happiness stems from feeling comfortable knowing that I will continue to deepen my understanding—even as my body ages and perhaps responds, or does not respond, in ways that are foreign to me now—of what it means to move in a body, connected to mind and spirit. If I had to say one thing from a physical standpoint—and this of course also requires adequate mental attention—it would be that I would like to continue to become softer (more water, less rock), holding a lesser degree of unnecessary tension throughout my body for longer periods of time, and therefore inviting in more ease of movement and experience, even while developing or maintaining muscle proved to be helpful in sustaining strength and balance in old age.

Along with this, I'd like to further establish my connection to my center—living from my heart, but moving from my center—the area two inches below the navel in the center of the abdomen—and in doing so experience the continual fluidity and strength of movement available to one who operates from their center point. Picture (or Google) a tai chi master, how fluid their movements are. This is an area of power, ease, and elegance available—in varying degrees—to us all.

Overall, I have found that when a greater sense of presence and ease entered me, along with it came peace and "less static," and I was able to see more, sense more, and appreciate more.

All these things helped my walk—and my life—become freer, deeper, and more meaningful.

As you go forth in your day, and your walks, ask yourself when are you rock and when are you water. Aim for water: flow, ease, openness, and expansiveness. I am not asking you to fully dismiss "the rock"—as it has value—nor to become fully "the water." What I am asking you to do is to discover when you are which—and also to know that the choice is always there. As always, awareness is key.

4

Some of My Favorite Walks

WHAT FOLLOWS ARE MEMORIES of my favorite walks throughout the years—some listed because of the company I was keeping, others because of the location—along with walking places I return to over and over because they either light something up inside me or send me deeper into my heart, or both. May what is shared here spark in you whatever may need to be realized, felt, or explored.

Walking in LA When It Rained

I lived in Los Angeles for twenty years. During that period, it rained ten times. Just kidding: we had many rainy(ish) winter seasons over the years along with some occasional summer showers and even a few genuine, bone-rattling claps of thunder. And pretty much each time the rain graced our city, I would go outside and walk, taking in the now-glistening trees, plants, flowers, and grass, the revitalized colors, the reactivated scents, the puddles, and the cleansed structures, along with breathing in the highly charged, fresh air.

Being that many Angelinos do not walk outside, or do much of anything outside, when it rains, people (in cars) would often pull over to ask "Are you okay?" or "Is everything all right?" assuming that my car must have broken down, or perhaps I'd been in an accident. So you see, it really is the City of Angels, and people in LA really do care—they just don't like getting wet.

On these rainy days, I'd often return home to a voice mail message from my friend Michael. It would go something like this: "It's raining. You're probably out walking. Call me back when the sun's out."

Of course I like to walk when the sun is out as well. (But do try the Rain Walk on page 74. It really is good for you.)

Walking the Coastline in Malibu, California

I would often walk along the beaches of Malibu. And when doing so with others, I would frequently tell (or remind) those accompanying me that for the majority of people in our world, this—walking along such a picturesque coastline—would only be a dream scenario, and that they may never see anything as beautiful or reach a destination such as this. And here we were, walking it; so let's see it, feel it, tune into it, enjoy it, and give something back to it—namely, *our presence.*

There are many things I like about walking along the ocean: the air (charged with negative ions), the sand and stones (grounding me), the water (often rushing in and retreating), the wildlife—both in and out of the water—the expansiveness, and how much it opens me up to possibilities and infinity in general, and of course the sound. But mostly, it is the aliveness of it all, and the ever-changing nature of it. The beach is never the same from day to day.

Again, we notice these things if we allow and train ourselves to be present to them. When we pay attention, the natural world has much to share with us. I am grateful for all that this spectacular stretch of coastline has shared with me, including the curious seals that would often follow along watching me as I walked the beach.

Walking among the
Giant Redwood Trees in Muir Woods

Muir Woods National Monument in Mill Valley, California, is a grove of coastal redwoods, the tallest of all living things on earth, and is one of the reasons I made the move from Southern California to Marin County.

There are moments when weaving through these majestic trees along the hillside ridge—while walking a path that overlooks the groomed walkways on the forest floor below—that I feel like I can fly. This feeling is so strong that I actually wonder, why can't I?

There is another powerful thing that I experience, beyond the sheer beauty of these trees that stand more than 300 feet tall and average 600–700 years old. There is an area called Cathedral Grove. It is a designated "quiet area." The energy is so still, serene, one could certainly call it sacred. And nearly every time I've walked through this section of the forest, my hand goes to my heart and stays there until I exit.

This hand-to-heart occurrence is not something I do consciously. It just happens. I look down, and it's there, resting on my heart. Perhaps you've experienced similar occurrences when you've allowed yourself to be deeply moved by a space you inhabit, or as in my case here, share with truly majestic tree-beings. That's the power of nature ... and presence.

Is there any place that makes you feel like you can fly or brings your hand to your heart? If so, I suggest you spend time there. And if you have not yet discovered such a place, I encourage you to be open to discovering one.

Walking with My Mother
in North Malibu, California

I once saw a Japanese film titled *After Life*, which had a very interesting premise: before moving on to the afterlife, you paused at a weigh station where you had to choose a favorite memory from your life—a memory that you would then carry throughout eternity.

Upon watching the film, I recalled a walk that my mother and I took one late summer day along the coastline in North Malibu. We must have walked two or three miles each way on what was a stunningly beautiful day. If ever there was a perfect walk, it was this one. And to this day, it is among my greatest memories, and I would be happy to live it out again and again through eternity.

What is your favorite memory?

Walking in New York City

As you may have gathered by now, I spend a great deal of time in nature, and I feel many of the world's problems could be solved, slowed, and/or further understood if we restored our connection with the natural world.

Having said this, for me, New York City is pure awesomeness. Amid all the life and energy swirling around, I often feel as if I am in some sort of grand opera. It's a perfectly chaotic space that allows me to expand outside my comfort zones, deepen my presence, further hone my awareness and realize (over and over) that "I" am not in control of this opera, and ultimately see and experience sights, sounds, and smells that dazzle, stir, and at times, challenge, my senses.

Having grown up in neighboring New Jersey, I have known the various boroughs of New York since my childhood, often going there with my family. But experiencing NYC later in life has been completely unique.

The first thing I do when I enter the city is center and ground myself and gather my energy to be sure that I am fully present in my space. (See the GBS Pre-Walk Check-In on page 46.)

I find that if one is not ready for cities such as these, it can be like being bounced around in a pinball machine—you being the ball. And it can also be very draining.

Once I am grounded, centered, and feeling fully embodied and present, I enter the flow, and often enjoy letting go ... and being the pinball, or the latest drop of water entering a fast-moving, multifingered stream.

If you want to test and grow your awareness skills and practices, take them into a bustling city (but first read about Crowd Walking on page 172).

Walking the Farmland in Norway

My mother grew up on a farm in southern Norway. I've had the good fortune to visit the land multiple times in my youth and also as an adult.

For me, it's incredibly special, almost indescribable, to walk these grounds, touching the trees (knowing some of them were just tiny when my mother was a child), feeling the earth, and smelling the scents.

Interestingly, one of the things that I first noticed about Muir Woods, near where I live here in Northern California, is that it smelled very similar to the forestland in southern Norway. I'm not sure why this is, but perhaps it has to do with the soil composition and the abundance of moss noticeable in each place, and the moisture as well.

Have you walked the grounds of those who came before you? If not, and it's possible to do so, I recommend it. It may be the perfect place to engage in the Seeing Walk (page 158) or Gratitude Walk (page 151).

Walking on Mt. Shasta

There are many places that light me up. Places that inspire me, teach me, confirm something for me, or challenge me to grow in all the best ways. But there is one place on earth that I'd call my spiritual home, my place of deep belonging, remembrance, and connection, and that is Mt. Shasta—a volcanic mountain that stands just over 14,000 feet at its peak—in Northern California.

There is much spiritual lore surrounding Mt. Shasta. For many, the mountain is like a magnet that draws or calls them to it. And there is plenty out there to read, or Google, or watch on YouTube, about the mystical side of Mt. Shasta. But I will say this: it's just plain beautiful. Pristine, refreshing, and restorative.

There are so many spots on and around the mountain that I love to take in through walking. Upper and Lower Panther Meadows are two of my go-tos.

There is a small window of time each year—usually mid-July to late September—when the snow has melted, and no new snow has yet arrived, when you can access Upper and Lower Panther Meadows.

With its soothing streams, wildflowers, Dr. Seuss-like spiraling trees, breathtaking views of the mountain, and its tremendous stillness, this is a heaven on earth type of feel. And walking slowly through these two meadows, joined by a short forest walk, is for many a life-changing—or at the least, life-affirming—experience. I've found myself mesmerized, left standing still as a stone, many times in these meadows.

If you're on Mt. Shasta in the summer, I encourage you to walk these meadows, accessed from Everitt Memorial Highway. Take these walks in any manner that moves you, but I especially recommend the Childlike Wonder Walk on page 224, Barefoot Grounding Walk on page 70, and Listening Walk on page 89. And please do so with the utmost respect for the delicate plants and wildflowers. They will appreciate your caring.

Walking along Outpost Drive

As I mentioned earlier, I lived in Los Angeles for twenty years. For much of that time I resided in the Hollywood Hills area. There was a loop walk that crossed back and forth across Outpost Drive, which led to the somewhat-famous Mulholland Drive, a highlight for many tourists because of its fantastic views of Los Angeles and the Hollywood sign.

I estimate I walked this loop a couple thousand times over the years. I always enjoyed looking at the houses, trees, flowers, cars, plants, and of course, connecting with the neighborhood people, including game show host Bob Barker, whom I would often pass while he was on his daily walk.

To this day, I remember each tree, curb stone, buckle in the sidewalk caused by tree roots, and rosebush along this just-under-a-mile walk. But what makes it most special and memorable are the friends who accompanied me on this walk: the conversations we had, the feelings expressed, the inspiration, dreams, fears, frustrations, and victories shared, and how much I and others grew during this period—on these short but deeply rewarding walks in this small pocket of Hollywood.

Is there a walk that you have done over and over that is somehow special to you?

The Pace of Others

Lastly, I'll share that what lives most special in me is having the chance in this lifetime to walk with others. And one of the things I've enjoyed the most over the years has been adjusting my pace to the pace of those I am walking beside. As I mentioned earlier, I'm six-foot-three; my stride is long (however, by nature I'm not an exceptionally fast walker), so it's always fun—and revealing for me—to meet the pace of others.

When doing so, I feel as if I am, in a sense, "walking in their shoes"—or at least their rhythm. I like the connection and the heightened awareness it brings me. Ideally, we want to settle into a pace that will serve everyone. But do take some moments to try on the pace of those you're walking with. You can do so during one of the group or two-person walks in this book, including the Working and Walking Things Out Walk (page 205).

And if you're reading this, and have walked with me, thank you for "your walk." I assure you it taught me a lot. And if you're one of the many "speedy walkers" I've walked with over the years, thanks for honoring my often less-than-zippy, "sorry-there's-another-rose-I-must-smell," pace as well.

A Walk I'd Like to Do

My father grew up in Berlin, Germany. As a young boy, he would spend much of his summers visiting his grandparents' farm in East Prussia (what is now Poland).

Because of modern technology, namely Google Earth, my father was able to share with me the exact spot where my great-grandparents' farmhouse existed, along with the rest of the small village. Interestingly, even though it's been more than seventy-five years since my father was there, almost nothing has changed.

When we viewed the zoomed-in satellite images, we could even spot the path he and his sister used to walk on through a wooded area (still intact) to reach a small nearby lake, which is also still there.

Of all the walks I have not yet taken in my life, this one tops my list. I would love to be back on that land and walk the same path and grounds that my father walked as a boy. I may even take a dip in the lake. Or walk in dedication to my father (see Dedication Walk, page 137).

Whatever the case, in this rapidly changing, developing world, I find it heartwarming to know that there are still areas on this planet that remain as they were years ago.

Is there any place you'd like to experience that has special meaning to you? If so, I encourage you to go there.

5

Before You Walk

WHAT FOLLOWS ARE GUIDELINES and tips to consider, along with instructions to implement, prior to embarking on your walks. This information will add dimension and clarity to your walks and will help you to get the most out of them. At the end of this chapter, you will find a GBS Pre-Walk Check-In, which I encourage you to perform prior to each walk.

Your Environment

Walking can be done anywhere—including on an indoor track if need be—and many of the walks described later in this book do not need a special environment; some can even be done in your home, like Walking Awake through Your Living Space (page 65). (See the list of walks in chapter 6 and the "Which Walks to Do When" Guide on page 231 to select your ideal time and location for each walk.)

Your current environment may not lend itself to comfortable outdoor walks. Perhaps you do not feel safe and secure walking in your neighborhood. You can always walk with a buddy, and when possible walk during daylight hours, but you may also want to search out surrounding areas (a park or an alternate neighborhood) that allow you to walk without worry. This is important, as you want to make yourself available to relaxation and ease rather than being on guard.

Weather

Certain types of weather may not always make an outdoor walk an option, although don't let a bit of rain deter you from being outside (see Rain Walk on page 74). High temperatures, snow, ice, etc., may prove challenging for the type of walking you will be doing.

Proper Clothing

The majority of the walks featured in this book are not designed to get your heart rate up and make you sweat—although you can certainly incorporate some of them into your more vigorous walks. So although you may feel energized and enlivened when engaging in many of the walks, your body may not be producing an abundance of heat. This is good to keep in mind when considering clothing.

You'll want to be comfortable. In cooler weather, dress warmly, but not too warmly. Layered clothing is always a good idea. Stay covered to the degree in which you are comfortable when walking in direct sun. (Even though the sun has a great many health benefits, for those who are sun sensitive, I suggest you wear light clothing covering you along with a hat or cap.)

For those walking at night, especially in areas of passing automotive traffic, I recommend that you wear bright reflective clothing or attach reflectors to your clothing. It's good to be seen—even when you are paying attention to your surroundings.

Footwear

Comfortable footwear is helpful. Whenever possible, try to walk in footwear that fits properly and is supportive. And try to avoid heels, but rather allow your feet to be as close to earth contact and natural function as possible.

High heels force you out of alignment from head to toe, caus-ing stress and imbalances on the feet, ankles, calves, knees, hips, low back, and quadriceps (thighs), and all the way up to your head. So in general, wearing heels works against the body's natural organization. Wear them occasionally for enjoyment, special occasions, or when fashion appropriate, but be mindful of their overall impact on your body—and limit or omit their use when engaging in any of the body awareness walks featured in this book.

Barefoot Walking

You'll discover that some of the walks presented later in this book rec-ommend barefoot walking (most specifically the Barefoot Grounding Walk, page 70). Of course you must be mindful of the terrain and the tenderness of your feet (as explained later, you may need to ease into it), but the benefits of reconnecting with your feet in this manner and then connecting them directly to the ground/earth are far-reaching: starting with the most basic, physical benefits, such as strengthen-ing, stretching, and reengaging the muscles, tendons, and ligaments in your feet. You'll also draw electrons up from the earth. Electrons are known to reduce free radicals (unstable atoms that can damage cells, causing illness and disease) in your body.

Hydration

Whether you're walking or not, hydration is important. There are many formulas available that tell us how much water to drink daily—half your body weight in ounces appears to be the most common. Find the amount that works for you, and make water your go-to choice to keep you well hydrated.

As far as hydration/water applies to the walks found in this book, again, the majority of the walks featured here are not of the draining, strenuous type. Having said this, you still may wish to bring water along with you, especially if it is hot or humid where you find yourself walking.

Distance

When considering the walks and concepts featured in this book, think quality over quantity, or presence over distance. Remember, when dealing with mindfulness and increasing awareness, less truly can be more. Unless you have a specific health and/or exercise goal that aligns with one of the walks, the amount of distance you cover during the majority of these walks is not of high importance. So try not to focus on the end destination or the completion of the walk (except when called for); just take one step, followed by the next step, and so on. What is important is how present and available you are to your body, your mental intention (when called for), and your surroundings.

File this under *tips for mindful awareness walking:* Taking ten steps when you are present is of more value than taking ten thousand steps when you are absent (tuned-out, in a rush, overthinking, fragmented in your focus, etc.).

Terrain

Depending on where you reside and what walking area is available to you, you will be walking on various terrains: on sidewalks, roads, and streets, and other times on paths, grass, sand, and perhaps even snow. Be mindful of shifting and varying surfaces, and know that all of these surfaces can—and often do—change from day to day. As you go deeper into the process of movement and walking, allow your awareness of the earth below your feet also to continually deepen.

Treadmills

For many of you, walking may be mostly done on a treadmill. As much as I encourage you to get out and explore, I realize that this may not always be possible or available. Because of this, I have included in your "Which Walks to Do When" Guide (page 231) a selection of the thirty-five walks that will serve you best while treadmill walking.

Cellphones

Technology can be our best friend, and technology can also be the biggest party pooper of our lives. It interrupts our own story, interrupts our ability to have a thought or a daydream, to imagine something wonderful because we're too busy bridging the walk from the cafeteria back to the office on the cell phone.

—STEVEN SPIELBERG

Can you leave your home or office and walk without a cellphone in your hand, pocket, or purse? It seems to be an impossibility. So I'm letting you know now that I may ask this of you at times, if for no other reason than to help you break (or temporarily disengage) from a habit and fear. Of course, if you are a caregiver or are in another must-be-reachable situation, use your best judgment.

Smartphones are fantastic. A dear friend of mine calls hers her "magic wand" because what these small devices can deliver to us is just that mind-blowing and bordering on magic. You may even be reading or listening to this book on one. But along with this magic often comes, among other things, a shortened attention span, increased distraction, stress, exposure to varying degrees of EMF radiation, "text neck" (yes, it's actually becoming a thing), and an addictive "comforting," often filling in for a sense of loneliness, emptiness, or boredom, as we get caught in a nearly never-ending dopamine (a neurotransmitter that helps control the brain's reward and pleasure centers) loop, where we just need more and more. Remember these words: Control your technology. Don't let your technology control you.

And don't worry, your cellphone's airplane mode setting will serve you greatly for the majority of the featured walks.

Reversing Your Route

By simply reversing the route of your regular, routine walk (for those who go in a loop, and not a there and back walk), you can change up your experience and grow your awareness significantly. First ask yourself, why do you favor this habitual direction to start with? It could be due to the way traffic flows, or the way a sidewalk is accessible, or it could be that you've never even thought about it—and would now enjoy going the opposite direction. If safe, look to reverse it. And allow in a new experience.

Nature

In every walk with nature
one receives far more than he seeks.

—JOHN MUIR

There are endless quotes pointing us to the gifts we receive from nature. I see the above quote whenever I enter Muir Woods here in Northern California. And for me, it has proved itself to be true, time and time again.

Whether it be for reducing stress (a study by Harvard Business School and Stanford University Graduate School of Business published in 2015 found that work-related stress accounts for up to $190 billion in health-care costs each year), elevating mood, lowering blood pressure, clearing our heads, absorbing negative ions from the air, or free-radical scavenging electrons from the ground, studies (and our own lived experiences) continue to show us how beneficial it is to get outside into nature.

And for me, it goes even deeper. Remember, we *are* nature. The connection is real and profound. And a large percentage of us are far removed from nature.

Many of the walks shared in this book revolve around being in nature. I realize that this may not be something that you are used to or comfortable with. You may have grown up in a city, with little connection to the natural world. Or you might just find nature to be too unpredictable, or you don't like bugs, or you just "don't get it," or whatever. That's fine. Everything in this book is to be done at your own pace and comfort level. But do consider the benefits. And *do* stretch and grow yourself.

File this under *forest food for thought:* The Japanese have taken the lead in developing and encouraging a practice called *shinrin-yoku,* which translates roughly to "forest bathing," which is a simple and profound practice of immersing yourself in the natural world. Forest bathing, also known as forest therapy, is not a strenuous practice, and it does not necessarily have anything to do with getting into water; rather, it is a way for you to bathe yourself in the natural world; walk quietly on a path; touch and smell flowers; lie down in a meadow; or hug, lean against, or smell a tree.

As for smelling trees, researchers have been studying compounds known as phytoncides that trees release into the air, such as the smell of cedar, for their promising health benefits, including the reduction of stress hormones, and enhanced activity of white blood cells.

I have a feeling we'll be hearing quite a bit about forest bathing in the coming years, including its ability to naturally boost our immune system.

Imagination

Our imagination is very powerful. So powerful, in fact, that our body chemistry often reacts the same to an imagined (or envisioned) event as it does to an event that actually occurs in our physical reality. Remember what I shared earlier about my foot floating effortlessly up while visualizing it doing so during the ankle exercise I described?

For years, athletes have experienced that imagining (visualizing in their mind's eye) themselves going through the motion, be it shooting a basket, shooting an arrow, clearing a hurdle, etc., will have nearly the same outcome as physically practicing these motions.

An experiment done by Australian psychologist Alan Richardson proved this to be true. In his study, Richardson chose three groups of students at random to perform basketball free throws. All of them were new to the practice of visualization.

Group one practiced free throws every day for twenty days. Groups two and three performed free throws on the first day and the twentieth day. But members of the third group spent twenty minutes every day *visualizing* free throws, right down to how the ball felt in their hands.

On the twentieth day, Richardson measured the percentage of improvement in each group. The group that practiced daily improved 24 percent. The second group, unsurprisingly, did not improve at all. The third group, which had physically practiced no more than the second, did 23 percent better, just shy of matching the group that physically practiced every day.

Going beyond the sports world, NASA also uses visualization—or what they call Visual Motor Rehearsal—with their astronauts.

I bring this up to instill in you the understanding of just how powerful our mind (and imagination) is. And how when we layer it into a specific walk, as we will often do in the walks to come, the effects can lead to very real experiences and outcomes both in your body and in what you may be wishing to accomplish, *draw to you, release,* or *better understand* in the outer world.

Our imagination can also set us free from the constraints and limitations of our linear mind and allow us to, if only for a brief and glorious moment, fly.

So remember all this as you engage in the walks that ask you to use your imagination or mental focus.

Your GBS Pre-Walk Check-In

Just as you find and gather your keys, wallet, purse, cellphone, etc., prior to exiting your living space, I want you to develop the conscious habit of finding these three other essentials: the ground beneath you, the breath within you, and the space around you.

Ground, breath, and space: GBS.

You'll accomplish this by using a three-step GBS Pre-Walk Check-In. Many of us have come to rely on a GPS (Global Positioning System) when traveling. Consider GBS to be your own *personal* positioning system. Developing this check-in practice will not only help bring you into the present prior to your walks; it will also help you to better inhabit moments and transitions throughout your day. This check-in will generally take less than three minutes and will eventually become second nature. When you're caught in the energy of your day, even just thinking these GBS steps will prove helpful: (1) Feel the Connection of Your Feet to the Ground, (2) Find Your Breath, and (3) Sense the Space around You.

STEP 1. FEEL THE CONNECTION
OF YOUR FEET TO THE GROUND

It's preferable to do this in bare feet or socks, but it's fine to do in shoes. While standing with your feet shoulder-width apart, feel the contact of your feet to the ground. Shift your weight from side to side and front to back, engaging the ground beneath you with different parts of your feet, then settle into a centered position, and root your feet into the ground.

Once you've established this rooted connection, you're going to slowly move your focus upward, as if taking an elevator ride up through your body. Starting at the bottom of your feet, fill your body with attention, never losing contact and connection to the ground—as if the ground is growing you—feeling awareness fill each part of your body, allowing your spine to lengthen upward until your neck is long and your head is high.

STEP 2. FIND YOUR BREATH

Tune into your breath, and bring it back under your conscious direction. Throughout this process, allow your body and mind to relax, letting go of burdens, stress, and tension.

Take three focused breaths, inhaling through your nose and exhaling through your mouth. (Aim to expand your belly and side ribs on the inhale, but don't force it.) For each breath, *inhale for four seconds, hold for four seconds, exhale for four or more seconds,* then *pause for four seconds.* Then allow yourself to feel your body breathing naturally.

STEP 3. SENSE THE SPACE AROUND YOU

Now that you've connected to the ground, sensed and grown your body upward, and harnessed and worked with your breath, focus on the last step: *sense the space around you.*

Even though it will often be willingly shared, and at times intruded upon, consider this your *personal space.* Often we are totally unaware of the space around us.

Using your mind, your imagination, or any other feeling/sensing faculties you may have, with your eyes open or closed, feel into and fill out the space immediately around you, three to five feet in each direction—in front and in back, to the left and right, below and above.

You may wish to think of your body being surrounded by an energy field, *your* energy field.

And for those of you who have had direct experience with the human energy field, or what some may refer to as the aura, you can consider this also an exercise in connecting with this element of yourself. See your energy full, clear, and vibrant around you. Envision it extending five feet out from you in each direction: front, back, up, down, left side, right side.

6

The Walks

WHAT FOLLOWS ARE THE thirty-five main walks. Each walk includes the following sections: Overview, Benefits, When to Do, How to Do, and Takeaways and Reflections.

Many, if not all, of the walks have a theme. I encourage you to go by "feel," fun, or at times, necessity, when selecting which walk you choose for yourself, your family, or your walking group.

Of course you may discover your own benefits, and I encourage you to do so. Let my words be a starting point, and never an end point.

There's a good chance that some of these walks and practices may stir up challenging thoughts, emotions, or realizations as you grow in awareness and as layers are peeled back. Don't fear this, but rather embrace it. And as always, practice self-compassion. Don't forget, breath is always there for you. Use it.

As you'll see, much of this is mental and has to do with setting intentions and engaging your imagination. Although the walks have overlaps and similarities—especially the visual-based walks—your task is to focus on the specifics and nuances of each one.

Almost all of the walks presented in this book can be done alone or in groups and may include suggestions on how to do them as a group.

However, a few of the walks in this book have more specific instructions for groups. These walks are the Listening Walk (page 89), Seeing Walk (page 158), and Gratitude Walk (page 151).

Some of the walks and their instructions may appear to be more spiritual in nature. This may be the case, but remember: they are all presented with the goal of deepening your physical life experience— whatever else ripples out (or in) naturally from this is to be viewed as an added benefit. Feel free to change some of my words to what may better align with your beliefs and what works best for you.

You will see that I mention times or moments in your life—both in the When to Do section of each walk and in the "Which Walks to Do When" Guide—when each walk may be appropriate, but the choice is always yours to make, and I encourage you to mix it up and expose yourself to every walk listed.

Also, you will see that at times I recommend combining elements of walks. An example is implementing a soft gaze while doing some of the visual-based walks and other walks. I encourage you to also feel free to combine and layer walks. For instance, you may want to do the Inner Smile Walk (page 82) in combination with the Barefoot Grounding Walk (page 70), or the Outer Smile Walk (page 85) in combination with the Gratitude Walk (page 151). But the key here is not to make things too complicated for yourself. So first do the individual walks, as presented, before combining and layering elements of them; and when you're inspired to combine them, do so!

A suggestion regarding these walks and children: Unless you as the adult feel strongly that there is a specific walk that you would like your child or children to do, I find it most productive to let them pick the walk themselves. Very often, if kids are shown something in a book, it suddenly becomes "official," or "cool," or seems to carry more weight and worth than when mentioned by a parent or other adult. So let them pick.

Lastly, some of these walks may at first seem ridiculous to you— and some may *always* seem ridiculous. That's fine. Just select what speaks to you. And realize that, as with all things, what may seem ridiculous to you may be someone else's absolute favorite, or most beneficial, walk. Such is life.

As far as repetition goes, many of these walks and their results tend to deepen for us as we do them over time. With that said, think presence over perfection, use your GBS Pre-Walk Check-In (page 46), and enjoy!

WALK 1   Heel to Toe and Toe to Heel Balance Walks

WALK 2   Turning and Tilting Your Head Balance Walk

WALK 3   Walking Awake through Your Living Space

WALK 4   Barefoot Grounding Walk

WALK 5   Rain Walk

WALK 6   Water Walk

WALK 7   Inner Smile Walk

WALK 8   Outer Smile Walk

WALK 9   Listening Walk

WALK 10   Making the World (or at Least Your Neighborhood) a Cleaner Place Walk

WALK 11   Walking Meditation (There and Back Style)

WALK 12   Walking Meditation (Circle Style)

WALK 13   Walking Meditation (Walking the Labyrinth)

WALK 14   Destination-Manifestation Walk

WALK 15   Earth Below, Heavens Above Walk

WALK 16   Full Moon Walk

WALK 17   Mindfully Walking Your Dog Walk

WALK 18   Forgiving Others Walk

WALK 19   Forgiving Yourself Walk

WALK 20   Dedication Walk

WALK 21   Prayer Walk

WALK 22 Affirmation Walk

WALK 23 Gratitude Walk

WALK 24 Seeing Walk

WALK 25 Centering Walk (a.k.a. Walking from Your Center)

WALK 26 Crowd Walking

WALK 27 Slow-Fast Walk

WALK 28 Slow Motion Walk

WALK 29 Soft Gaze Walk

WALK 30 Backward Walk

WALK 31 Grieving Walk

WALK 32 Working and Walking Things Out Walk

WALK 33 Head, Heart, Hara Walk

WALK 34 Seeing from Different Parts of Your Body Walk

WALK 35 Childlike Wonder Walk

WALK I
Heel to Toe and Toe to Heel Balance Walks

Next to love, balance is the most important thing.

—JOHN WOODEN

OVERVIEW

Balance in all its many forms and expressions is about more than just *physical* balance. Balance can be experienced in all aspects of your life, from your relationships with others, to the way you consume food, drink, and media, to the way your mind works. All elements of balance are important. And many of us see the need for our *overall balance* to become more refined as we mature, both mentally and physically.

While the Heel to Toe and Toe to Heel Balance Walks, along with the Turning and Tilting Your Head Balance Walk (page 61), are primarily included here for you to better connect with and build upon your physical balance, they are also here—and this may occur instantaneously or over time—to reveal to you where you may be out of balance, beyond just the physical expression of the word: where and how you may be off-center, holding yourself back, caught in between decisions or directions, or simply unaware of the balances and imbalances within your life and world.

One example may be how you stand your ground, or do not stand your ground. Things to ponder: Does your life feel balanced? What does a balanced life look like to you? What does it feel like? What shift can you make, or what action step can you take, that might cause your life to come more into balance?

Granted, maybe we'll never lead fully balanced lives—if such a thing even exists—but we can all discover where the imbalances are, and start to make the shift into better equilibrium.

Like all the walks featured in this book, the balance-building/balance-revealing walks are an invitation into deeper awareness and layers of self-discovery, and they are particularly beneficial for bringing us into the present moment. And ... I think they are fun to do.

Having said that, be aware that frustration may arise when you are challenged by these walks. A beneficial mindset is to think of this more as *play* than as work or exercise or something to perfect. Allow yourself to soften. Breathe. Challenge yourself, but don't beat yourself up. Think: less rock, more water.

These walks engage and challenge the brain in a way that helps it create new neural pathways. You may find that the wobble in your balance begins to steadily improve as you develop new pathways to assist in carrying out the task.

I suggest, especially at first, performing the Heel to Toe and Toe to Heel Balance Walks in the order presented; the given order is generally experienced as *less difficult to most difficult.*

> NOTE   If you are balance-challenged, unsure of yourself, or dealing with injury, be sure to have someone at your side to spot you, or at the very least do these walks beside a wall or other fixed object, like a countertop, that can be easily relied upon if needed. Consult your wellness provider if you have severe or increasingly challenging balance issues.

For those of you who wish to improve your relationship to balance, consider these affirmations: "My balance is getting better and better." Or "In all areas of my life and being, my balance improves daily." And for those who find greater benefit by confirming it fully in the now, try: "My balance is perfect." Whether silent or aloud, repeat your chosen affirmation throughout your day. You may wish to include visualizations with these affirmations.

If you already feel confident in your ability to execute these walks, your job is to make their execution more and more refined and elegant. Think: *poetry in motion.* And remember, you can never have *too good* balance.

Moshé Feldenkrais often said the following when describing what he and his students and teachers were setting out to do. You'll see here how it applies to challenging walks and newly explored movement: "It is our focus to make the impossible possible, the possible easy, and the easy elegant." After performing and getting better at the Heel to Toe and Toe to Heel Balance Walks, you will see how much easier regular walking becomes, and how the easy becomes "elegant."

As time goes on, think of this walking technique, and how you were able to do it, and improve, as you walk regularly through "unbalanced" situations.

BENEFITS

- Strengthens and restores physical balance.
- Improves coordination.
- Brings you into the present.
- Grows proprioception (awareness of the position of your body in space).
- Helps you to gain focus.
- Has the potential to reveal to you where you may be "out of balance" in your life.
- Stimulates your brain and creates new neural pathways.
- Helps children to become centered, focused, and calm. *This is a great physical exercise to incorporate into a bigger lesson or discussion when teaching children about balance.*

WHEN TO DO

- Can be performed once or twice a day.
- When desiring to increase balance.
- When wanting to stimulate your brain.
- When feeling the need to explore larger balance issues in your life.
- When needing to slow down.

- When wanting to increase focus.

- When needing to accomplish something (especially great for children in this regard).

- When feeling bored.

- For groups to use as a supportive, trust-building exercise between individuals as they take turns supporting (spotting) and encouraging one another as well as offering helpful feedback.

- For those adventurous, inquisitive types, you may wish to try these Heel to Toe and Toe to Heel Balance Walks when you are feeling angry, sad, joyful, confused, or any other mental or emotional state, just to see the difference—if any—in your balance and the outcome. (Consider this as yet another way to get you off autopilot and see and *feel* deeper into your lived experience.)

HOW TO DO

Forward Balancing Walk: Heel to Toe Walks

a. HEEL TO TOE WALK—LOOKING AT YOUR FEET

Find an even surface that will allow you to take ten to fifteen steps in a straight line, be it an existing seam or line on the floor or carpet, or a piece of masking tape that you apply to the floor. If outdoors, and feeling safe and confident, you can use the lines in an empty parking lot or even the lines in many sidewalks. Be sure to clear the space of any potential tripping hazards.

When possible, perform in bare feet. Otherwise, perform in comfortable, secure, and supportive shoes.

After you've performed the Heel to Toe and Toe to Heel Balance Walks as instructed here, revisit them with your attention dropped down into your center (see the Centering Walk, page 165) and see if you notice a difference in your balance.

Turn off your cellphone, switch it to airplane mode, or leave it behind.

Perform your GBS Pre-Walk Check-In.

Begin by putting one foot directly in front of the other, *with the heel of the front foot touching or close to touching the toes of the back foot.* (If you find it too difficult or uncomfortable to bring your feet to touching or nearly touching, then bring them as close together as you comfortably can.)

Stand this way for ten to fifteen seconds, remaining connected to your breath, before proceeding. Prior to taking your first step, you may want to visualize yourself moving forward—and later backward—in a balanced manner.

While looking down at your feet, take ten to fifteen deliberate, heel to toe steps. Then turn around and repeat, as many times as you feel comfortable.

Holding your arms out to the side can often help with balance. But first try the walk with your arms resting at your sides. Some people also find it centering to do this walk with their hands placed palms-together in prayer position at the chest/heart level. (I recommend this variation for kids, as it really does seem to center them.)

After you complete this portion of the walk, walk back and forth in your normal gait and see how it feels.

b. HEEL TO TOE WALK—LOOKING FORWARD

Begin your walk in the same manner as described in exercise a. This time, keep your chin up, parallel to the ground, and your eyes looking forward. You may wish to find and focus on a fixed spot straight ahead, but also allow yourself to "sense" your surroundings via your peripheral vision.

Step forward, bringing the heel of your back foot to just in front of, or touching, your front foot. (If you find it too difficult or uncomfortable to bring your feet to touching or nearly touching, then bring them as close together as you comfortably can.)

Take ten to fifteen heel to toe steps. Then turn around and repeat, as many times as you feel comfortable.

After you complete this portion of the walk, walk back and forth in your normal gait and see how it feels.

C. HEEL TO TOE WALK—EYES CLOSED

Be sure to use a partner to stand beside you or to hold your hand for this exercise.

Begin your walk in the same manner as described in exercise a. This time, keep your eyes closed.

Go slowly. Remain connected to your breath. Rely on your partner or spotter if need be. And remember, your goal is to be present, *not perfect.*

Take ten to fifteen heel to toe steps. Then turn around and repeat. And then repeat again. You can of course do less.

After you complete this portion of the walk, open your eyes and walk back and forth in your normal gait and see how it feels.

Backward Balancing Walk: Toe to Heel Walks

You may find these to be more challenging than the forward variations. If you are unsure of your balance or are recovering from an injury, you may wish to have a spotter for these exercises, or do these walks next to a wall or another fixed object.

d. BACKWARD TOE TO HEEL WALK—LOOKING AT YOUR FEET

Turn off your cellphone, switch it to airplane mode, or leave it behind.

Perform your GBS Pre-Walk Check-In.

Then take one foot and place it directly behind the other—the toes now touching or close to touching the heel. (If you find it too difficult or uncomfortable to bring your feet to touching or nearly touching, then bring them as close together as you comfortably can.)

If you can, hold this position for ten to fifteen seconds, stabilizing yourself as you remain connected to your breath.

Next, look down at your feet and begin to walk backward—toe to heel—for ten to fifteen steps. Then turn around and repeat, as many times as you feel comfortable.

Make your steps as fluid and deliberate as you can. You can hold your arms out to the sides or in prayer position at the chest/heart level for stability, or just let your arms hang naturally.

After you complete this portion of the walk, walk back and forth in your normal gait and see how it feels.

e. BACKWARD TOE TO HEEL WALK–LOOKING FORWARD

Begin your walk in the same manner as described in exercise d. This time, you will be looking forward as you move backward. Take ten to fifteen toe to heel steps. Then turn around and repeat, as many times as you feel comfortable.

After you complete this portion of the walk, walk back and forth in your normal gait and see how it feels.

f. BACKWARD TOE TO HEEL WALK–EYES CLOSED

Be sure to use a partner to stand beside you or to hold your hand for this exercise.

Begin your walk in the same manner as described in exercise d. This time, keep your eyes closed.

Begin to walk backward—toe to heel—for ten to fifteen steps.

Take your time, breathe, recognize and release any tensions that arise, and move deliberately. Rely on your partner if need be. Your goal is to be present, *not perfect*.

Then turn around and repeat, as many times as you feel comfortable.

After you complete this portion of the walk, walk back and forth in your normal gait and see how it feels.

TAKEAWAYS AND REFLECTIONS

What was your experience like while doing the Heel to Toe and Toe to Heel Balance Walks?

If you have completed more than one variation, or perhaps all of them, did you prefer one variation over another? Which did you find most challenging? Which was easiest? Which do you feel served you best?

Did anything you experienced surprise you? Did you find yourself breathing freely, or were you holding or grasping at your breath as your balance was challenged? If you weren't very challenged by the walks, could you make the movements elegant?

Think about and perhaps jot down any takeaways and reflections you may have. You may first want to concentrate purely on what you experienced in the physical sense: "I was wobbly," "I tilted more to one side," "My shoulders became tense," "It was weird to close my eyes and try to walk," etc.

Then examine the mental aspect: Did any thoughts come up during the walk that may have affected it one way or another? (Oftentimes, there may be critical thoughts of self-judgment.) Did any specific thoughts negatively affect your balance? For example: you thought of your job, your to-do list, or something else that seemed to coincide with your misstep or sense of non-sure-footedness.

Conversely, were there any thoughts that were present when you were performing the exercise with more ease? Were there moments when you had no thoughts at all?

Did a song come to mind that helped you with your balance? I mention this because some people have shared with me that they heard a certain song in their head that helped them remain more sure-footed and less tense while performing their balance walks. Perhaps you too have a balance song, or prayer, or mantra that is waiting to be called upon.

WALK 2

Turning and Tilting Your Head Balance Walk

There is balance within the wind, within the sea, and within you. Find it.

—DIANA GAZES

OVERVIEW

Like the Heel to Toe and Toe to Heel Balance Walks, the Turning and Tilting Your Head Balance Walk is a commonly prescribed walk to improve balance. I am placing it here as yet another way for you to discover where your balance may be lacking, and as a tool to help you grow/improve not only your balance, but also your connection to your body.

Some may find the Turning and Tilting Your Head Balance Walk to be easy to execute, whereas others may find themselves weaving quite a bit and unable to manage a straight walk during certain head positions.

For those who find it easy, your task is to make it elegant, fluid … poetry in motion.

For those who find it difficult, your job is to go easy on yourself, and to realize that increasing and restoring balance is a process. Have fun with it. Remain lighthearted. And as always, *breathe*.

If at any moment, you find yourself getting dizzy, stop the walk.

Just as I encouraged you to explore balance beyond just physical balance while approaching the Heel to Toe and Toe to Heel Balance Walks, I invite you to do the same here.

And remember, you can never have *too good* balance.

BENEFITS

- Increases balance.
- Grows proprioception (awareness of the position of your body in space).
- Stimulates your brain.

- Reveals which head movements and positions are more apt to take you off your center while walking.

- Provides an opportunity to find more freedom and ease in your neck and head throughout the turning/movement process.

- Allows you to see and feel the connection of the body from head to toe in ways that may be unique to you.

- Challenges you in new and beneficial ways.

WHEN TO DO

- When in need of improving balance.

- When wanting to grow bodily awareness.

- When wanting to experience your everyday walk in a new and unique way.

- When feeling the need to explore larger balance issues in your life.

NOTE   It has been my experience that this walk has the ability to work quite deeply into your system; therefore, it's recommended to do only once per day.

HOW TO DO

Find a space outdoors, or wherever else affords you a clear, preferably level, space where you can walk a hundred or so feet without any potential tripping hazards.

If you are balance-challenged, unsure of yourself, or dealing with injury, be sure to have someone at your side to spot you during the Turning and Tilting Your Head Balance Walk. And consult your wellness provider if you have severe or increasingly challenging balance issues.

Turn off your cellphone, switch it to airplane mode, or leave it behind.

Practice the following movements before you begin walking: Turn your head to your right. Turn your head to your left. Look up. Look down. Tilt your head to the right by bringing your right ear toward your right shoulder. Tilt your head to the left by bringing your left ear toward your left shoulder. These are the movements you will be performing during your walk.

Perform your GBS Pre-Walk Check-In.

Begin to walk in a straight line, or as straight a line as you can, for a hundred or so feet.

Every other step, *look to the left and then look to the right.* Do this six to ten times.

Then every other step, *look up and then look down.* Do this six to ten times.

Then every other step, *tilt your head to the left and then tilt your head to the right.* Do this six to ten times.

Try to remain as fluid and "tuned-in" as possible. Never strain or force the movement of your head. Look for where you can reduce tension, and become aware of which position or movement either causes you discomfort or challenges your balance.

Stay connected to your breath, and feel your feet on the ground.

Remain aware of your thoughts, and what arises in you, including any self-judgment.

After completing the walk, walk normally and see how you feel. You may even want to repeat the same distance and line, but now do it as you normally walk: your chin parallel to the ground, and your eyes looking forward.

TAKEAWAYS AND REFLECTIONS

What was the Turning and Tilting Your Head Balance Walk like for you? Was it easier than you expected? Was it harder than you expected? Did you feel challenged in any way that surprised you? Did you notice if any of the movements pulled you off your straight line? For example, perhaps each time you looked left or down, you felt yourself sway.

Were there tensions in your neck or elsewhere in your body that revealed themselves? Were you able to soften any of these tensions?

Did you find yourself breathing freely, or were you holding or grasping at your breath?

Did any emotions come up? Any revelations? Were you able to concentrate? If not, what kept you from concentrating?

Jot down or make mental notes of any takeaways and reflections you may have, and work with these discoveries as you continue to explore the Turning and Tilting Your Head Balance Walk.

Lastly, realize that you're doing great.

WALK 3
Walking Awake through Your Living Space

The best way to capture moments is to pay attention. This is how we cultivate mindfulness. Mindfulness means being awake. It means knowing what you are doing.

—JON KABAT-ZINN

OVERVIEW

This may seem like an odd name for a walk, since unless we're sleep-walking, we're always awake as we walk through our living space. But I have a feeling you may know where I'm going with this.

Each day we travel through our living space, and unless we have just moved in, have recently redecorated, had a flood or other disaster, or have a real sense of presence, for the most part it soon becomes a blur.

And by a blur I mean that things have become below our conscious radar—we pass items en route to other items; for example, grabbing the television remote from the end table, but never noticing the end table if it were not for the remote placed atop it.

Part of this is the brain's way of shielding us from overload, and part of this is that we have become, in a sense, asleep to our environment, as we are at the same time moving at our, often very distracted, speed of modern life.

Walking Awake through Your Living Space can reveal quite a bit. Whether these discoveries prove to be large or small, it is always beneficial to do a deep check-in with the place we call home. And it is indeed an ongoing process.

For some of you, "walking awake" through your living space may not be an experience you're looking forward to, as the last thing you may want to do is really see and feel your living space. All the more reason to embark on this walk/exercise. *Remember, awareness is the first step to change.*

And at the forefront one must remain grateful. Encouraging you to have gratitude for your home environment—and the fact that you have a roof over your head—is important to me, but I know gratitude does not always come easy. At least agree now to let the seeds of gratitude take root within you—and within your living space.

BENEFITS

- You get a chance to connect with the place you call home in a way that you may not often, if ever, do.

- You get to see, hear, smell, touch, and sense what makes you feel light and inspired, open and expansive, comfortable, and supported—versus heavy, uninspired, closed off, uncomfortable, and unsupported.

- You get to discover what changes you would like to make, or feel called to make, in your space and yourself.

- You gain a greater appreciation for the space you live in, and a better understanding of what may or may not be working for you anymore.

- For partners and families, this is a chance to evaluate if the space still meets everyone's likes and needs.

- This is a great walk/exercise for kids to participate in as well, though it's good to set guidelines for children who participate in this walk. You can start by asking them to find, share, or discover their favorite spot or spots, their favorite items perhaps, and where they feel the calmest and most comfortable.

- It sparks creativity.

WHEN TO DO

- When desiring to, or needing to, deepen your connection to your living space.

- When taking stock of your life.

- When feeling the need for change, not just in your space, but outside your space as well.

- After an event that has caused or is causing a deep shift in you: a divorce, a marriage, the passing of a loved one, the birth of a child, the leaving of a child (empty nest), a new job, a new direction, or falling in love.

- When feeling the need to sell or give away unused items, or items that no longer inspire or serve you.

- When looking to declutter and lighten the overall energy of your living space.

- When curious to see what every moment of your life has now led up to.

- And of course, pick a "when to do" time when you will have the least distractions.

HOW TO DO

Turn off your TV, shut down your computer, and reduce or eliminate any other potential distractions that are within your power to reduce, including your phone.

Perform your GBS Pre-Walk Check-In. With this specific walk, give extra focus to the last step, "sense the space around you." You may wish to carry a notebook and a pen to jot down any thoughts that arise for you, or you may wish to just keep a mental list.

You may choose to set an intention prior to beginning. An example may be: "I will now see, hear, feel, and sense anything in my living space that needs to be seen, heard, felt, or sensed for my highest good and the highest good of all."

For those aligned with prayer, you can say a prayer asking that "all that needs to be revealed within my living space shall be revealed to me."

For those of a critical nature, remember to only be as critical as is productive.

Pick a direction and start to move through your living space in the most present and aware state of mind that you can be in, with all your senses alive and activated.

Moving slowly and deliberately, look at everything, from the structure of the space itself—high ceilings, low ceilings—to the doors and doorways and the windows and floors—to each item: the rugs, carpets, light fixtures, decorations, furniture, appliances, books, linens, etc.

Allow yourself to stop where you feel compelled to stop, look where you feel compelled to look, touch, feel, smell, and listen. Do you hear anything you haven't heard before?

Notice the colors. Notice the lighting. The lack of lighting. The dust. The areas that are clean. The areas that could benefit from cleaning. The areas you love but spend too little time in.

Run your hands across items you do not normally touch, or perhaps have not touched in months or even years.

See how each item, object, color, or specific space feels to you as you give it your full attention. What do you need to see?

Notice the space between items, and the lack of space. Notice what makes you smile and feel good—again, allow gratitude in—and notice what makes you feel not so good.

Do you have an absolutely favorite spot?

Do you have a place where you feel the most centered? The most alive? The most inspired? The calmest? The strongest? The most you? Do you spend time in this area or areas?

How is your sleeping space? Is your bed in a position you prefer?

Continue to feel your feet making contact with the floor as you move through your space.

Know that your mind may be triggered to go in many directions, heading off into thoughts, old memories, maybe some judgments. Explore them briefly. Then use your breath and the feeling of your feet connected to the ground to return to the present.

Conclude your walk when you have covered the amount of space that feels right.

TAKEAWAYS AND REFLECTIONS

What did you learn from Walking Awake through Your Living Space? Did anything surprise you? Confuse you? Inspire, or spark, something within you?

How does your living space make you feel—in body, mind, and spirit? Are there changes that you'd like to make? Was gratitude present for you? Are there items within your living space that you are ready to part with?

If you have not already done so, make a mental list of, or jot down, your experience(s) having walked awake through your living space.

Remember, the purpose of your living space is not only to provide safety and shelter, but also to make you feel good: healthy, inspired, refreshed, balanced, centered. If you're not there now, do what you can to take the steps to get yourself there.

Know that seemingly tiny changes or movements—like placing items in areas that feel better to you, or allowing in more light, or even changing the type of lightbulb—can have deep and lasting effects on your mood, attitude, and overall well-being.

Repeat this walk every so often, and see what comes up. In the meantime, stay awake to your living space ... and the world.

WALK 4
Barefoot Grounding Walk

You learn a lot when you're barefoot.
The first thing is every step you take is different.

—MICHAEL FRANTI

OVERVIEW

How often do your bare feet connect with the natural world?

In this day and age, many of us go years without allowing our naked feet to come in contact with the earth—be it a beach, a forest path, an area of inviting grass, or the soft bed of a gently flowing stream.

I realize that for some, due to injury or ongoing pain from problematic feet, walking barefoot is nearly or entirely out of the question. But for the majority of us, it's not. And somehow spending time being barefoot has become odd, whereas walking in high heels has become normal.

You must be mindful of the terrain and the tenderness of your feet while walking barefoot. But you also must be mindful (and informed) of the benefits of reconnecting with your feet in this manner and then connecting them directly to the ground/earth. The benefits are great: starting with the most basic physical benefits, such as strengthening, stretching, and reengaging the muscles, tendons, and ligaments in your feet—to the drawing up of electrons from the earth—electrons which then aid in neutralizing free radicals in the body.

For many, barefoot walking (and what has become known as "earthing") has completely transformed their lives.

There are numerous testimonials in which people describe improvements in sleep, lowered blood pressure, reduced inflammation, increased mental clarity, reduced pain, and reduced stress—all from this simple act of connecting their bare feet to the earth.

So much so that "earthing" has now become a "thing" and is being researched and studied for its many benefits.

On top of this, sometimes we are so "in our heads" that we feel disconnected from our body. A Barefoot Grounding Walk can be a quick antidote for this.

BENEFITS

- Grounds you.
- Calms you.
- Helps you to focus.
- Can improve balance and posture.
- Connects you to nature and the energy of the earth, allowing you to absorb electrons through the soles of your feet.
- Helps get you out of your head and into full embodiment.
- Exercises, strengthens, stimulates, and often *reawakens* areas of your feet that have long been held captive by the confining and contorting shapes and styles of shoes.
- May help reduce blood pressure.
- Lastly, those into the practice of reflexology believe that there are specific points on the feet that correspond with organs and systems of the body. Because of this, they often prescribe walking barefoot to stimulate these "pressure points" in your feet.

WHEN TO DO

- When feeling overwhelmed, "scatterbrained," or too much in your head.
- When needing to feel grounded.
- After spending a lot of time using electronics.
- When feeling sluggish or low energy.
- When needing life to slow down.

- When wanting to strengthen and stimulate your feet, and allow them to breathe.

- When wanting to connect your energy to the energy of the earth.

- When wanting to improve balance.

- Feel free to give it a try for some of the reasons mentioned in the Overview, including improved sleep, reduced inflammation, and lowered stress. You may be surprised by your own positive results.

NOTE Where not to do: You'll want to avoid areas, predominantly cities, where there is a strong ground current due to underground electrical wires. For the most part, you will not encounter this in more natural settings.

HOW TO DO

As you can imagine, a Barefoot Grounding Walk is really quite a simple practice, without any significant challenges, besides the tenderness you may initially experience when connecting your naked feet to the earth.

First, select your location. Be it a beach, trail, park, field, forest, or your own backyard, it should be inviting. If walking on grass, you may want to check if the grass has recently been treated with anything that may be toxic, like pesticides.

Turn off your cellphone, switch it to airplane mode, or leave it behind.

In bare feet, perform your GBS Pre-Walk Check-In, really feeling your feet connected to, or "rooted" in, the earth—and the ground growing you upward.

Then simply choose a direction and begin your walk.

Enjoy the sensations. Feel the connection. Discover areas of your feet—and how they perform for you—that may have long gone unnoticed.

Pause every now and then to wiggle and spread your toes, root yourself in the ground, and see if you can sense or feel the energy and aliveness of the earth.

Remain mindful. Be present. Pay attention to how your whole body feels, including your posture and balance, as you walk barefoot.

Permit yourself to come fully alive. Laugh. Smile. Play. Breathe.

Take some steps with your eyes closed, and see how it feels to you.

And if you find a space that feels really feet-friendly, and you'd like to ramp up your pace and elevate your heart rate—that's great as well. But be sure to remain aware of your body—its feelings and sensations—and your surroundings even while going faster. (See Slow-Fast Walk, page 178.)

Also, the simple act of *standing*—with no movement—on the naked earth can be highly beneficial, so keep that in mind when you need a quick, focusing, grounding hit of earth.

At the conclusion of your walk, or when first returning to wearing footwear, allow yourself to tune in and feel the difference from the bottom of your feet to the top of your head as you walk.

And in the words of Woods Hutchinson, let us remember: "Everything, from kings to cabbages, needs a root in the soil somewhere."

TAKEAWAYS AND REFLECTIONS

If you are not accustomed to walking barefoot outdoors, how did it feel? Was it relaxing? Energizing? Stimulating? Fun? Did any unique thoughts or emotions arise in you? Did you feel more connected to the earth, or sense anything that hinted at a connection to something grander?

How did it affect your balance and posture?

Jot down or make mental notes of any takeaways and reflections, then continue to track them as you further engage in your practice of barefoot grounding/earthing walks in the various locations that call to you.

WALK 5
Rain Walk

Rain is grace; rain is the sky descending to the earth; without rain, there would be no life.

—JOHN UPDIKE

OVERVIEW

For you, rain may not be grace; but there is no denying that without rain, there would be no life. And so begins a long list of all the good that rain brings to us, can reveal to us, and allows us to experience.

Unless you live in an area such as Seattle, with its high levels of rainfall that are nearly impossible not to engage with, you may try your best to avoid being outdoors when it rains. Maybe it depresses you, or you were told from a young age that being out in the rain will make you sick (not true, but getting chilled can lower immune function), or you just don't like the idea of getting wet.

A Rain Walk done on your own terms—not when you miss your bus, or are wearing your favorite shoes or clothes, or are in other ways ill-prepared or inconvenienced—can be a highly enjoyable experience. *If* you allow it to be.

As I mentioned in chapter 4, "Some of My Favorite Walks," going for a walk in the rain is one of my favorite things to do. The trees, plants, flowers, and grass all come alive. Objects begin to glisten. Colors are revitalized, scents are reactivated, streams are reborn, structures are cleansed, puddles (fun to study your reflection in, walk through, or stomp in) are formed, and the world looks different.

And then there's the air. The air becomes fresh and charged with negative ions.

What is a negative ion? Negative ions are oxygen atoms charged with an extra electron that you inhale in abundance in certain natural environments, such as mountains, waterfalls, forests, and beaches. Among other "positive" attributes, negative ions are known to counter various forms of pollution (including what your computers and other electronics give off) and airborne allergens, and are believed to produce biochemical reactions within the body that raise levels of serotonin, which contributes to your overall well-being and happiness.

Negative ions are also present in the air during and after a rainfall.

Science aside, I've also found that walking in the rain can bring out a genuine sense of joy and playfulness in people. This is so important in a world that seems to be getting increasingly swallowed up in stress and seriousness.

By the way, children tend to love the Rain Walk—especially when we adults encourage creativity and playfulness as opposed to trying to control their every move.

BENEFITS

- Opens you to experiencing the world around you in ways that you do not often experience.

- Invites fresh air and stress-reducing negative ions into your body.

- Encourages playfulness, exploration, and all the good that comes from not being so serious, including rekindling your relationship to the child within.

- Provides you with a greater appreciation for nonrainy days.

- And … you may encounter a rainbow.

A quick story: One rainy day I could not locate my umbrella. So I purchased a new, very inexpensive one from a nearby convenience store. I left the store and immediately opened the umbrella to the rain. Much to my delight, the sound I heard when the rain struck the surface of this far-from-designer umbrella was wondrous. It was as if I had won the umbrella lottery—for under $5—and each raindrop brought with it the most beautiful music. And it kept me dry. Perfect.

WHEN TO DO

NOTE Even though the experience can be beautiful and dramatic, for safety reasons please avoid performing your Rain Walk during a thunderstorm.

- When wanting to explore and appreciate your surroundings in a newly experienced manner.
- When feeling the need to relax, let go, and play a bit.
- When wanting to allow yourself—or your walking group—to be part of earth's cleansing and restoration process, perhaps experiencing firsthand the quote from above: "Rain is grace; rain is the sky descending to the earth; without rain, there would be no life."
- When wanting to connect to the child within you.
- Whether it be during the buildup to the rain (when the air is becoming charged) or during the rainfall (when the world around you is being cleansed and nourished) or soon after the rain (when negative ions fill the air), gift yourself a Rain Walk.

HOW TO DO

First, dress appropriately. This by no means is meant to put a damper on your desire to be clothing-free or minimally clothed when appropriate.

Pick a location that is familiar to you—and experience it in a new and dynamic manner—or head to a location that you feel may be wonderful/wonder-filled during a rain shower.

You may choose to bring an umbrella. You may also choose to go barefoot.

Turn off your cellphone, switch it to airplane mode, or leave it behind.

Perform your GBS Pre-Walk Check-In either before or after heading outside.

Begin your walk. Do so with your eyes, ears, nose, and all your other sense organs fully activated and engaged.

Notice raindrops on leaves, or street signs, or car mirrors, or anywhere else you can discover them.

Remain connected to the ground, and be mindfully aware of—and curious about—the snails, slugs, worms, and other life-forms that often emerge during rainfall.

Observe puddles forming, note reflections in them, stomp, stand, or dance in them. Look at the sky; feel the rain on your face, your hands, your smile.

Notice the reactivated streams and the direction of the newly flowing water on the ground.

Breathe the air. Invite in the negative ions. Say thank you. Smile. Laugh. Walk faster, then slower. Stand still. Notice.

And if so inclined, sing!

Remember, this rain you're experiencing is part of an ongoing cycle that sustains all of life, including yours.

Conclude your walk. If chilled at all, be sure to take measures to warm yourself.

TAKEAWAYS AND REFLECTIONS

What did you notice from your Rain Walk? Were you already a rain walker? Or was this a new or relatively new experience for you? Did you do it alone or with others? How did it make you feel?

What are some of the takeaways and reflections stirred within you from walking in the rain? Are you looking forward to walking in the rain in other locations? Did a location come to mind where you'd like to walk in the rain? Can you think of one now?

Jot down or make mental notes of any takeaways and reflections that may come to mind.

WALK 6
Water Walk

They both listened silently to the water, which to them was not just water, but the voice of life, the voice of Being, the voice of perpetual Becoming.

—HERMANN HESSE

OVERVIEW

The Water Walk is about walking near water. Whether it be the ocean, sea, a creek, stream, river, lake, canal, or waterfall, there is something very powerful about walking in the presence of water, be it fast-moving or seemingly still.

Part of this felt power stems from our deep connection. (The earth and a newborn baby are both approximately 71 percent water.) So you can see the connection: just like the earth, we are mostly water.

What do we receive when walking near bodies of water? For each of us it may be different, but the words that come to mind for myself and many who have come before me are: inspiration, a sense of flow, awe, wonder, peace, calm, expansiveness, relaxation, infinity, direction, connection, ebb and flow, ease, a feeling that "everything will be okay," and the ability to settle down and breathe.

On top of this, there are the negative ions (learn more about negative ions in the Rain Walk, page 74).

BENEFITS

- As mentioned above, you are composed largely of water. Your connection to it, in its various shapes, forms, and expressions, has a deeply ingrained, if not always conscious, place within you.

- Being near water helps you to reconnect to yourself. It can inspire, heal, and balance you.

- Provides an opportunity to see and experience a large aspect of the planet you call home, and opens you to a grander vision and version of yourself.

- Tends to bring you into the present, often helping you to "simply be" or get "back into the flow."

- Grounds you, relaxes you, and recharges you.

- Allows you to absorb nature's health-enhancing negative ions.

WHEN TO DO

- Engage in the Water Walk whenever you can.

- When you need to calm yourself or clear your head: a still body of water can be very helpful.

- When you seek inspiration, or outward motivation, or need to relax, recharge, and reconnect to something larger than yourself: an ocean, a waterfall, or a mountain lake can serve you well.

- When you wish to open up and release any stagnant aspects of yourself or your life, or remind yourself that it's okay to surrender and "go with the flow": a flowing body of water, be it a creek, stream, or river, can be highly beneficial.

- When you need to dream, or to expand beyond your current limited vision: the oceans and seas of the world await you.

HOW TO DO

Decide on your location. For those living in urban areas that may not lend themselves to many water choices, try to find a stream, a pond, a river, or other body of water nearby (a quick internet search can be very helpful in this regard), or travel a distance to expand your options.

Turn off your cellphone, switch it to airplane mode, or leave it behind.

Perform your GBS Pre-Walk Check-In.

Set an intention for what you would like to receive from this location's walk. Examples may be: "I would like to let go of my past hurts." "I will now allow inspiration to enter me." "I will leave here more peaceful than when I arrived." "I will no longer feel small." "I will once again find my flow."

Then begin your walk in a way that aligns and feels connected with your intention or desire for this day or this moment.

Allow yourself to be present, to listen, to see, hear, and feel the water—at times physically touching it and at other times just letting it figuratively wash through you. Use your imagination; see and feel yourself receiving what you need from the water, and from this walk.

Allow emotions to arise. Allow inspiration, clarity, and understanding.

Feel your feet on the ground. Remain aware of your steps, your movements, your breath.

Allow yourself to move/walk at a pace that transcends your everyday, habitual walking pace, and rather becomes something more aligned with the moment, received from the water in front of or beside you.

Relax your jaw, neck, shoulders, and arms; allow yourself to surrender any "rock-like" parts, patterns, or habits that no longer serve you; and embrace the "water" that is there to help you on your path.

Conclude your walk knowing that you are now a different, or at least a renewed, person.

TAKEAWAYS AND REFLECTIONS

There are many forms and bodies of water to walk beside. I'm sure you will experience variations of them in your own perfect timing. My advice is to allow yourself to continue to open to what arises in you when you encounter the various manifestations of water found on our planet.

What have you experienced while walking near water? What have you learned? What have you let go of? What have you embraced? Did anything surprise you? Did anything challenge you? Did anything make you say "Yes!"?

Do you feel that you have a greater connection to water after consciously and mindfully walking beside it?

Do you have any favorite memories from moments spent walking in the presence of water?

The biggest takeaway you can give yourself from the Water Walk is to know that, like the water itself, you are beautiful and you are needed.

WALK 7
Inner Smile Walk

Sun gives light; torch gives light, candle gives light; smiling gives light.

—MEHMET MURAT İldan

OVERVIEW

The Inner Smile Walk is one of my favorite walks. I find it is not only potentially profound for mind-body connection, but it also just feels so good to do. Kids love it, too.

It's a walk that brings us into our body in a way that brightens it, bone by bone, organ by organ, muscle by muscle. It's a way to move through our being with a warmth and love, and a smile.

And it's pretty much guaranteed to make you feel brighter—and often lighter—from the inside out. I've found that when I perform the Inner Smile Walk, an outer smile forms on my face.

BENEFITS

- The Inner Smile Walk allows you to travel through the inside of your body, along with the surface of your body, in a way that you probably never have. Through the mind-body link, it helps you develop a deep connection to spaces recognized and unrecognized in your body.

- It warms and brightens your insides, and spills over to your outsides.

- You get to pinpoint areas of your body and bathe them with deep love and appreciation.

- It lights up your brain and can create new neural pathways.

- Its very nature is gratitude.

- I can't prove it, but I believe healings take place.

WHEN TO DO

- Whenever you could use an "internal boost," or when you feel the need to connect deeper into your body in a loving, uplifting way.

- When certain ailments or situations prompt you to do so.

- When you wish to stimulate your brain and strengthen your mind-body connection.

- This may also be a walk that feels right to do every day for a duration of time that feels good, and effective, to you.

HOW TO DO

Pick your location.

Turn off your cellphone, switch it to airplane mode, or leave it behind.

Perform your GBS Pre-Walk Check-In.

Envision the smile you are going to move throughout your body. It can be a traditional "smiley face" or any other uplifting smile that springs to mind. (Some people have also found it beneficial to use the image of a glowing sun.)

Begin your walk.

As you walk, envision this internal smile placed throughout your body. Begin anywhere in the body, and end anywhere.

For some, especially before a strong mind-body connection has been formed, it is helpful to place or *insert* the smile by hand into the different areas of your body while walking.

Keep the smile in any area you wish, or feel called to, for any duration of time or distance.

Then move it to another area. Move it in small or large jumps—from one place to the next—or let it glide along. For instance, picture the smile gliding down your arm, lighting up everything along the way, and ending in the palm of your hand. The smile can also travel through your bloodstream.

The smile can be large or small. So large as to fill up your entire back, or so small that it lives in a freckle.

For those who need a little more guidance, you may find it helpful to guide the smile up one side of the body and then down the other.

As mentioned above, you may wish to physically touch the area where you will envision the smile, and you may wish to insert the warm smile into an injured area, an area where you hold stress, or just an area that intuitively calls out to you.

Be sure to let it fill your brain, the area behind your eyes, your neck, your digestive system, your kidneys, your sexual organs. Try to envision the smile in each vertebra of your spine.

This all may be odd to do at first; but remember, there is no perfection with these walks; there is only presence. And the presence will deepen with time and practice.

And of course you can share this inner smile with those who come across your path, and you can even imagine/envision the smile being placed on or inserted into plants, trees, clouds, cars, buildings, houses, birds, and anything else that comes into your field of vision.

At the conclusion of your Inner Smile Walk, you may do whatever you wish with the smile. It can remain in an area of your body, it can become so large that it encompasses the all of you, or you can take it out and place it somewhere outside yourself, including releasing it into the air and sending it to someone or something you love, or out to the world at large.

TAKEAWAYS AND REFLECTIONS

What was your experience like while performing the Inner Smile Walk? Did anything surprise you or make you think or feel deeply about a certain body part or area? Could you place/envision and move the smile easily into certain areas and not as easily, or not at all, into other areas? Did you feel the area light up or "come alive" when the smile was placed there?

Jot down or make mental notes of your experiences, and then see how they shift, grow, and evolve as you continue to engage with the Inner Smile Walk.

WALK 8
Outer Smile Walk

We shall never know all the good that a simple smile can do.

—MOTHER TERESA

OVERVIEW

There's a saying: "When we smile, the whole world smiles back at us."

You may not have experienced this firsthand to such a degree, but I'm sure you have been on the giving or receiving end of a smile that has brightened your day or another person's day.

There are countless stories relating how a simple, well-timed smile has changed someone's day, and may have even given them the will and desire to keep on living.

What the Inner Smile Walk does for your insides, the Outer Smile Walk will do for the world outside of you (and of course it will always reflect back to you as well).

Meeting and acknowledging what's in front of you with a smile is a powerful practice.

Of course you must be mindful of the people and situations around you, but the world certainly needs more smiles. And if you can deliver them, and feel good in the process, do it.

Many of us do not like our smiles or are insecure about our smiles. Much of this is because we are often told via advertising that perfectly aligned and very white teeth are the key ingredients to a fabulous smile. I disagree with this. I feel, and have experienced, that a dazzling, moving smile begins deep within us. Even if we have a set of teeth that will never be featured in a toothpaste commercial, we can still light up the world with our genuine smile.

I myself grew up with crooked teeth and various dental appliances to make them better. I would not say that I was terribly insecure about my teeth, and I don't think I even gave much thought to my smile. But in the eighth grade something happened that really made me think (and feel good) and also proved the above point that our smile is more than our teeth.

It was the time in the school year when they asked students to vote on the physical and other attributes of the students (to be used later in the yearbook): "best dressed," "most athletic," "funniest," etc., along with "best smile."

On voting day, one of the most popular girls in my class came up to me and told me she voted for me for best smile. I remember being caught off guard, silently wondering if she was kidding. But she was sincere.

That moment taught me a great lesson. There I was with far from perfect teeth, and still someone saw the beauty or inner shine, or whatever she may have seen, coming through my smile.

BENEFITS

- Sharing a smile with whatever appears before your eyes is a powerful mechanism for spreading love, gratitude, and appreciation. It allows the world in front of you to be seen and acknowledged in a way it rarely is.

- It allows you to smile at objects you may have never thought to share your smile with.

- It helps you become more present to your environment.

- It helps children to embrace their smile and to more greatly appreciate the world that surrounds them.

- Smiling is good for you. Here's what studies on smiling have revealed: Smiling makes you feel good (by releasing endorphins and serotonin), reduces stress, boosts your immune system, elevates your mood, lowers your blood pressure, makes you more attractive to others, helps you remain positive, and makes you more approachable. Smiling is contagious. Even a manufactured smile produces these benefits.

WHEN TO DO

- Whenever you feel moved to share good with the world.
- When you wish to shift your mood into a better place, or pull yourself out of a funk.
- When wanting to make yourself a magnet to new connections, and not just of the human kind.
- When wanting to connect deeper to your neighborhood environment, or any other area you're drawn to.
- When you wish to show your appreciation for life, and maybe lower your blood pressure at the same time.

NOTE It may seem strange to smile for what on the surface appears to be no reason at all. But once you get in the groove, and your appreciation begins to grow, smiling becomes easier and less strange, and may even become second nature.

HOW TO DO

Choose your walking location. You can also perform the Outer Smile Walk within your living space, infusing everything with your appreciation.

Turn off your cellphone, switch it to airplane mode, or leave it behind.

Perform your GBS Pre-Walk Check-In.

Put on a smile. It does not have to be a full-blown "say cheese" style smile, but more a smile of appreciation. (Remember, it doesn't have to be perfect. It simply has to be yours.) Sometimes the deepest smiles take place mostly in your eyes.

Begin your walk.

Acknowledge everything your eyes land upon with a smile. Smile at a sidewalk, acknowledging that it gives you a place to walk. Smile at a building, because it provides shelter for whomever lives there. Smile at a telephone pole, because it helps keep us all connected. Smile at everything. Smile at the world. Smile your appreciation.

Allow smiles to come naturally as well. You may not normally smile at a mailbox (unless it's a pretty spectacular mailbox), but you may often smile at the sight of a flower. Allow these natural smiles to blend in with the smiles you are consciously serving up to things in the world you are encountering or focusing on.

Also, allow yourself to feel good, allow your mood to elevate, allow stress to dissipate, and allow your true essence, that part of you that is larger than your fears, doubts, insecurities, and any feelings of separateness, to shine through.

And of course, when appropriate, you can always share this smile with those who come across your path.

Conclude your Outer Smile Walk knowing that you showed up for the world in a unique and healthy way.

TAKEAWAYS AND REFLECTIONS

What did you learn from engaging in the Outer Smile Walk? Did it feel strange to you, or did it come somewhat easy? Was it odd to share your smile with nonhuman, nonanimal objects? Did anything surprise you? Did you perform it with others, or were you alone? Did it lift your mood?

Jot down or make mental notes of anything that arose from your Outer Smile Walk.

WALK 9
Listening Walk

The earth has music for those who listen.

—SOURCE UNKNOWN

OVERVIEW

Do you consider yourself a good listener? Do you see the value in listening? Have you had people in your life who modeled good listening for you?

Do you hear your surroundings? Do you listen to the world as you move through it? Can you distinguish between sounds you like and sounds you do not like?

The Listening Walk is a gift that gives to us on many levels, including interpersonal, interspecies, and relational to our environment.

I find that what we lack as a culture, we often lack as an individual. And listening, in our modern, fast-paced, often-distracted culture, appears to be a lost, or losing, art.

The Listening Walk is presented here as an antidote, and as a way for you to tune deeper into life.

Just as the majority of us are fortunate enough to be able to walk, the majority of us are also fortunate enough to be able to hear. Let's not squander this gift. Rather, let's use it to grow our awareness, our understanding, and our hearts.

You can do this walk with one or more other people if you would like to experience it as a shared or group experience. It's wonderful for families, siblings, teams, work groups, walking groups, and just about any other pairing you can come up with.

The Listening Walk for two or more people gives us a chance not only to "hear as a group" but also to experience the differences of what each individual may be naturally drawn to or tune into or be able to hear, versus what you or others in the group may be drawn to or tune into or be able to hear.

It's a perfect walk for large groups to perform—listening in unison, comparing notes in real time—or to perform as individuals who later compare notes. It's also great for two people to engage in in a more intimate, one-to-one manner.

I recommend you engage in this walk in any creative way that comes to mind, including "listening" to group listening ideas that others may present.

BENEFITS

- The Listening Walk is here to bring you into deeper relation with the world, to awaken, or strengthen, one of the core ways in which you receive information.

- It will grow you, teach you, and open you up to the world around you.

- If you are walking as a group, it will more deeply connect you and your group, revealing much through the act of individual and collective listening.

- It will help you and your group to locate the often-priceless silence between sounds.

- It is a tool, always at your disposal, that will bring you into the here and now, the present, no matter where you may find yourself.

WHEN TO DO

- Whenever you want to experience a location (be it indoors or outdoors) in a way that you may have not done before; namely, using hearing as your most focused-upon sense.

- In familiar spaces, in and around your home and neighborhood, or in other locations that either call to you (as "great listening spots") or you find yourself in.

- When you want to test your hearing, alone or as a group—tuning into sounds nearby or sounds far off, sounds with a low pitch or sounds with a high pitch.

- When you need to be on your own with the world.
- The Listening Walk is perfect for a child or children when they are bored or lacking focus or are waiting for something else to occur. Have them make a game out of how many unique sounds they can hear.

Allow for great variation:

- When it's calm and still or loud and teeming with life.
- In the midst of city sounds or in the midst of nature sounds.
- In the morning, the daytime, or the nighttime; when it rains, when it snows, when the wind blows, or when something in you, or in your walking partners, suddenly says, "I *must* hear that."

HOW TO DO: ALONE

You may wish to carry a notebook and a pen to make a "listening list" of sounds heard. You may even wish to set an intention of something you'd like to hear or become aware of.

Pick your starting point. As you consider Listening Walk locations, be sure to include your immediate surroundings and familiar areas that you may inhabit but have never actively listened to before.

Turn off your cellphone, switch it to airplane mode, or leave it behind.

Perform your GBS Pre-Walk Check-In.

Then take a moment to listen, starting with your own breath, and then to the sounds nearest to you.

Begin to walk.

Remember, these walks are not to a set or prescribed distance. You may end up walking many miles, if you so choose, or a few hundred feet, or perhaps only twenty feet (there is often a great deal to hear and sense in a twenty-foot space).

As you walk, listen. Don't "strain" to hear, but be "present" to hear.

Keep your eyes active and aware, but let your ears lead.

Let the pace and the walk be enjoyable.

Tune into which sounds are made by people, and which sounds are coming from the natural world.

Locate and identify the individual sounds that make up the layers of sounds around you. You may wish to determine which direction the sounds come from: *songbirds to my left, train horn behind me,* etc.

If you find a sound that you love or that intrigues you, stay with it. It's more than fine to pause your walk in order to tune in deeper.

If you wish to record a sound with your cellphone, or, as stated earlier, create a "listening list" of sounds heard, do so.

Realize that depending on where you are, you may go for long stretches without hearing anything new—or anything at all. When this is the case, appreciate the lull, and see if the silence would like to say anything to you.

You can also ask yourself: What don't I hear? Think of the sounds that are absent, or absent from your everyday life. (This is a great exercise for children, and also a powerful, revealing exercise for adults.)

Conclude your walk with a richer understanding of and deeper connection to your immediate surroundings or wherever you may have found yourself during your solo Listening Walk.

HOW TO DO: FOR TWO OR MORE PEOPLE

Choose a location that fits well with your Listening Walk for two or more people. Be sure to consider your immediate surroundings and familiar areas that you may inhabit but never actively listened to before. You may wish to decide upon the particulars of the walk, the route, distance, etc., prior to starting off, or you may choose to allow yourself to be led by the sounds.

You may each wish to carry a notebook and a pen to make a "listening list," or you may designate one individual from the group or pairing to note the collective sounds heard. (A listening list is a tremendous way to engage children. They love the immediate gratification of hearing a sound and then jotting it down.)

Consider setting a group intention of something you'd like to hear or become aware of. (For instance, the song of a bird that is known to be in the area, or another sound or sounds that may intrigue and interest the group.)

Turn off your cellphone, switch it to airplane mode, or leave it behind.

Perform your GBS Pre-Walk Check-In as a group.

Then take a moment to listen, starting with your own breath, and then to the sounds closest to you.

Begin to walk.

As you walk, listen. Don't "strain" to hear. But be "present" to hear.

Keep your eyes active and aware, but let your ears lead.

Let the pace and the walk be enjoyable and suit your family or group.

Tune into which sounds are made by people, and which sounds are coming from the natural world.

Locate and identify the individual sounds that make up the layers of sounds around you.

Become aware of what you can hear and identify versus what others in the group are hearing and identifying.

You may wish to call out a location or direction for each sound: "Songbirds to our left," "Train horn behind us," etc.

If your group finds a sound that they love or that intrigues them, stay with it. Remember, it's more than fine to pause your walk to tune in deeper.

With the help of another person at your side, you may wish to take turns walking for short distances with your eyes closed and see how this affects your hearing.

If you or others wish to record a sound with a cellphone, or create a "listening list" of sounds heard, do so.

Realize that depending on where you are, you may go for long stretches without hearing anything new—or anything at all. When this is the case, appreciate the lull, and see if the silence would like to say anything to you or the group.

You can also ask yourself and your fellow listeners: What don't you hear? Think of the sounds that are absent, or absent from your everyday life. (Again, this is a great exercise for children.)

When doing a there and back walk (not a loop but heading one way and then returning back the same way), I find it great to have kids listen to (and list) what they hear on the way out, and then concentrate on (and list) what they *do not hear* on the way back. For example, if they're in nature, they won't hear a TV, a video game, a cellphone, or other items whose sounds may have become woven into their everyday life. On the return journey, ask them, "What don't you hear?" Encourage them to write or verbally share a list.

Conclude your walk with a richer understanding of and deeper connection to your immediate surroundings or wherever you may have found yourself walking during your Listening Walk for two or more people.

TAKEAWAYS AND REFLECTIONS

Did anything surprise you about your Listening Walk? Did any sound or sounds land deep within you? Did you identify sounds you never heard before—even those within or around your own home or neighborhood? Did you discover a sound or sounds you love? A sound or sounds you dislike?

Would you say it was a noisy walk? A quiet walk? A stimulating walk? A revealing walk? An inspiring walk?

What types of emotions did you experience—inspiration, excitement, surprise?

If you went on the Listening Walk for two or more people, reflect on the following questions:

What did you learn as a group listening? What did you yourself learn?

How did performing the Listening Walk for two or more people bring benefit or greater awareness to you?

Was the group, be it two or twenty, able to remain present? Were there any interesting, revealing silences?

Did you or your group create a listening list featuring each of the unique sounds heard? Did your walking partners identify sounds different from yours?

I encourage you to jot down or make mental notes of any takeaways and reflections you may have, and continue to do so as you visit and "listen to" more and more spaces and places. And in your listening, let there be gratitude.

WALK 10
Making the World (or at Least Your Neighborhood) a Cleaner Place Walk

The best way to find yourself is to lose yourself in the service of others.

—MAHATMA GANDHI

OVERVIEW

I would like to add to Gandhi's quote: "and in the service of the planet."

I was uncertain about featuring this walk, and then I thought back to all the smiles of accomplishment I've witnessed over the years when accompanying people on cleanup walks or seeing photos of those who had just completed a cleanup walk.

There is something very rewarding and internally uplifting when we improve our environment.

This walk, whether done alone or as a group, has the potential to not only make a difference in your home surroundings, or wherever else you may choose to clean up, but make a difference inside you as well.

When asked what to do when feeling down, the Dalai Lama is known to respond with a simple sentence: "Try not to focus so much on your own self; rather, focus on helping or doing something for others."

I have seen the truth of his message/suggestion play out time and time again. When someone is feeling down, they can rise up out of it by doing something caring for others.

Grabbing a bag and cleaning up your neighborhood, or walking path, or parking lot, can truly make a difference in seen and unseen ways for you and those you are serving with this act of thoughtfulness.

Local hardware stores, gardening stores, home improvement stores, etc., have been known to sponsor group cleanups, providing bags, gloves, and other supplies. So you may wish to tell them what your intentions are and ask if they'd like to assist.

BENEFITS

- Beautifies your neighborhood or anywhere else you choose to clean.

- Allows you or your group, be it family, friends, or others, to experience making a noticeable difference in the world you live in.

- Lifts your spirits, and provides a sense of accomplishment born of simple service.

- Brings you into the present.

- Provides a great "actions speak louder than words" example for anyone who may witness your random act of caring and cleaning—including children.

- This is a great walk for kids to partake in, as long as they are well supervised and are interested in participating.

WHEN TO DO

- Whenever you are feeling down, bored, uninspired, or overly focused on yourself, or when you could use your own internal boost.

- When you wish to improve the surroundings near your own dwelling or others'. Or along your favorite path, at a local park, along a stretch of beach, or at a school.

- When overwhelmed by the larger wrongs of the world that seem out of reach and insurmountable, and wanting to make an immediate difference in a way you can.

- When wanting to lead by example.

HOW TO DO

First off, try to do this walk with an attitude of gratitude and loving service rather than anger. I say this because it is very easy to find our mood going dark and only wanting to judge others as we look at the various pieces of trash tossed about. In this moment of service, that anger serves no one, and only causes irritation in your own being.

So stick to the task at hand, and when doing so, you may be surprised at the number of would-be future litterers taking note of your actions.

Pick your location. Grab or purchase a sturdy trash bag and some gloves.

Some people also like to use a trash picker stick (a stick you can purchase or make, with a nail or something similar at the end to poke the trash with and then insert it in the bag) or a trash grabber stick (a stick with jaws at the end that works mechanically by use of a trigger-pull on the handle).

Perform your GBS Pre-Walk Check-In, because even when you head out with a specific task, you will still want to engage in it in a mindful, present manner.

Head off on your walk solo, or with family, friends, your regular walking group, or a newly formed "cleanup group."

Allow yourself to, as Gandhi said, find yourself in the service of others.

Gather up articles of trash and insert them into your bag. If you are walking with other people, you can take turns holding the bag.

Do not put yourself into precarious situations, examples being the side of a roadway with fast-moving traffic, or the slippery embankment of a river or canal, or any other location that causes you to take pause. As well intentioned as your heart and actions may be, it's not worth injuring yourself.

Remain mindfully aware of your body as you perform this walk. Be conscious of your feet on the ground, the space around you, your breathing, and your movements in general as you reach, bend, twist, and turn while gathering the individual items.

Pace yourself. Be present to the good you are doing.

Complete your walk and dispose of your items in the most appropriate way you can, including recycling the recyclables.

TAKEAWAYS AND REFLECTIONS

What are some of your takeaways and reflections from the Making the World (or at Least Your Neighborhood) a Cleaner Place Walk?

Did it make you feel better? Did you realize the good that you (and perhaps your group) did and the accomplishment itself? Were you disheartened by the amount of trash? Can you think of other places where you would like to perform this walk?

Jot down or mentally note your takeaways and reflections, and please take a moment to accept my appreciation and thanks. Even if it was one can that you removed, you have made the world a cleaner place.

Lastly, please never give up on humanity, and never give up on yourself. And I shall do the same.

WALK 11
Walking Meditation (There and Back Style)

The goal of meditation is not to get rid of thoughts or emotions. The goal is to become more aware of your thoughts and emotions and learn how to move through them without getting stuck.

—DR. PHILIPPE GOLDIN

OVERVIEW

As stated earlier, meditation has far-reaching benefits—be they physical, mental, or spiritual—and engaging in meditation is a profound way in which to come to better know ourselves. As Lao Tzu reminds us: "Knowing others is intelligence; knowing yourself is wisdom."

Since one of the key benefits of meditation is increased awareness, I consider all the walks presented in this book to be meditation walks. Having said that, walks 11 through 13 are specifically presented as more traditional meditation walks; the first two are variations of commonly known walking meditations, and the last is a labyrinth style meditation walk.

First, what is meditation? Dictionaries will often define it as contemplation; pondering; a mental exercise for focusing; examining attentively and deliberately.

All those definitions are accurate, but I find this definition from *The Free Dictionary* to sum it up well:

Meditation is a practice of concentrated focus upon a sound, object, visualization, the breath, movement, or attention itself in order to increase awareness of the present moment, reduce stress, promote relaxation, and enhance personal and spiritual growth.

Meditation, in all forms, is also a highly personal practice. Seated and lying meditation yields tremendous benefits, some that may not be obtainable via walking meditations; but walking meditation is a practice that translates extremely well to our everyday life (and walking through it), and I've found it highly beneficial for those who are physically limited in their ability to sit comfortably for extended periods, or are just not wired for doing so.

While walking meditation has been a deeply revered practice in spiritual traditions for centuries—be they Daoist, Sufi, Buddhist, Christian, or other—it is important to remember that (as Yoga International reminds us) "Meditation is not part of any religion: it is a science, which means that the process of meditation follows a particular order, has definite principles, and produces results that can be verified."

Meditation also helps to expand our consciousness beyond our everyday, seen, shared, and experienced reality, connecting us with— or into—a larger state or field of knowing.

For those who believe in God, a saying that is often shared is: "We speak to God in prayer. We listen to (or hear) God in meditation." One could also say we become more receptive to our intuition, or that still quiet voice within us, or the benefits of a clear and focused mind.

The Walking Meditation (There and Back Style) is a meditation practice that will allow you to continually refine and deepen your connection to yourself and your walk.

It is the perfect antidote for the go-go-go, overstimulated society in which the majority of us find ourselves living.

NOTE Partaking in walking meditation in public can at times appear odd to those in the surrounding area. Do not let this get to you. But also remain mindful of not drawing unnecessary attention to yourself; remember, you're not showing off, you're showing up. Conversely, I've found that people often become curious and at times ask to join in.

BENEFITS

- Reduces stress. Increases focus and concentration. Expands awareness. Centers you.
- Makes you available to the inspiration that is often born of quiet contemplation.
- Can reduce blood pressure.
- Brings you into the present.
- Helps children to focus and become centered.
- Invites a sense of inner peace and calm.

WHEN TO DO

- When in need of focusing and becoming present.
- After or during a stressful day.
- When wanting to quiet your mind.
- When looking for inspiration born of quiet contemplation.
- When wanting to connect with your body and breath in a centering, calming manner.
- When in need of inner peace.
- When feeling ungrounded.
- Before or after your seated meditation practice.

HOW TO DO

Begin by choosing a location that is quiet or relatively quiet with limited distractions where you can walk back and forth for fifteen to thirty feet. (A private space can help you to feel less self-conscious, but it is not needed.)

You can perform this walk indoors as well, which may at times, especially at first, be perfect for you; but remember, outdoor spaces, and spaces in nature, tend to add to or deepen the experience, allowing for greater concentration with fewer distractions than at home, along with the other benefits nature brings us.

Can be done barefoot when the location is appropriate.

Find a lane, line, or relatively straight path to walk. (Choose flat or relatively flat terrain, and avoid hills for this walk.)

Turn off your cellphone, switch it to airplane mode, or leave it behind.

Perform your GBS Pre-Walk Check-In. You may wish to set an intention or speak a prayer for what you would like to receive or release from your Walking Meditation (There and Back Style). Or you may wish to repeat, silently or aloud, an affirmation. Some examples are "As I walk, I am calm," "With each step I feel calmer and more centered," or simply "I am here."

You may also wish to speak to each footfall and each rising foot: As your foot touches the ground, say, "I have arrived." As your foot rises, say, "I move in the present."

Allow your arms to hang comfortably at your sides with your hands relaxed, or you may clasp your hands lightly in front of you, clasp them lightly behind you, or place them palms-together at your chest/heart level.

Walk at a pace that is slower than your normal pace, and take smaller steps than you are used to taking.

Keep your spine long, allow your shoulders to relax, and place your focus on the ground three to six feet in front of you.

Allow your eyes to relax, softening your gaze. (See the Soft Gaze Walk, page 191.)

Allow your face to become softer, which often begins with releasing any tension in your jaw.

Walk fifteen to thirty feet, *pause,* then turn around, *pause,* and walk back. (Remember, in meditation you arrive in each moment, so even though you are walking back and forth, "there and back," you are concentrating only on the step ... then the next step ... and the next.)

Remain aware, or continue to grow your awareness, of the ground beneath you, your body moving through space, your clothes moving on your body, and your breath.

When your mind wanders, bring it back by focusing on your breath and on your feet touching and releasing from the ground.

Just like thoughts, feelings and emotions may arise. Be with them. Don't fight to suppress them, but also realize that they do not define you but rather are something you are experiencing in this moment. It often helps to simply label them for what they are: "This is frustration," "This is anger," "This is fear," "This is clarity," "This is peace."

For variety, or when really feeling the need to get centered, you may wish to drop your attention down into your center, the space two inches below your navel in the center of you, and walk from this center point. (See the Centering Walk, page 165.)

Repeat this mindful, back and forth meditation walk for five to twenty minutes, remembering to pause at the completion of each pass.

Conclude your walk. Take a moment in stillness.

Remember, the principles of mindfulness and awareness meditation can be applied anytime. You can do this Walking Meditation in a regular—not there and back—manner at any time and at any location—even when walking through a shopping mall.

TAKEAWAYS AND REFLECTIONS

What was your Walking Meditation (There and Back Style) experience like? Were you able to slow your mind down and focus? Did you feel calmer or more at peace performing your Walking Meditation—or immediately after completing it? Do you feel more centered? Were you able to remain aware of your breath and the movement of your body through space?

Did you receive any insights, answers, epiphanies, or welcome ideas from your Walking Meditation?

Are you excited or inspired to share this Walking Meditation with others? Can you think of others who may benefit?

Jot down or make mental notes of any takeaways and reflections you may have, and continue the Walking Meditation (There and Back Style) whenever the need or desire arises.

WALK 12
Walking Meditation (Circle Style)

In the circle, the beginning and end are one.

—HERACLITUS

OVERVIEW

For some, there is no better way to get centered and feel "whole" again than walking a circle. It may sound odd—who walks in circles, right? But the Walking Meditation (Circle Style) is a practice that invites a natural focus, allows for deep concentration, and places us into a state of unbroken connectivity—namely, a circle.

Just as there are walking lanes or paths specifically designed for Walking Meditation, there are also circle paths created for the practice of "walking the quiet circle." You may not be able to visit monasteries, churches, cathedrals, Zen centers, or other spaces that offer these areas devoted to Walking Meditation, but you can find or create your own.

When we walk a circle, we can simply follow the way and more easily disengage the thinking mind, the critical mind, and just be present in the moment—with each step feeling our way and our wholeness.

A simple circle can be walked in your backyard or other available space that is accessible to you and allows you to feel comfortable while partaking in the Walking Meditation (Circle Style).

Although many people prefer to walk an empty circle, others choose to circle around a tree, a fountain, a pool, or whatever else can help them hold the circle.

BENEFITS

- Reduces stress.
- Increases focus and concentration
- Allows you to mentally unplug or detach from trying to figure anything (or *everything*) out, and rather to simply be as you walk the circle.

- Helps you to feel and reconnect with your wholeness.
- Grows your awareness.
- Settles your nervous system.
- Invites in inspiration, and answers born of inner stillness.

WHEN TO DO

- When in need of focusing.
- When feeling ungrounded.
- After or during a stressful day.
- When wanting to quiet your mind.
- When looking for inspiration born of quiet contemplation.
- When wanting to connect with your body and breath in a centering, calming manner.
- When in need of inner peace.
- When needing to accomplish something for yourself. Walking a circle is a great way to invite in "completion" or a sense of "wholeness."
- Before or after your seated meditation practice.

HOW TO DO

Find your circle space. The circle does not have to be overly large, but I would recommend at least six to eight feet in diameter. Many people walk around fountains, trees, pools, or other landmarks that lend themselves to being circled, but there is also something special about walking around a circle that is empty at its center. You can then fill it with your intentions, or what you may be leaving behind, or just allow for its emptiness.

Turn off your cellphone, switch it to airplane mode, or leave it behind.

Can be done barefoot when the location is appropriate.

Perform your GBS Pre-Walk Check-In.

You may choose to set a mental intention of what you'd like to receive prior to beginning the walk, or to repeat an affirmation while engaged in the walk. (For example, "As I walk this circle, I return to wholeness," "In body, mind, and spirit, I am whole and complete," or "I walk this circle in complete trust.") You may also speak a prayer.

Allow your arms to hang comfortably at your sides with your hands relaxed, or you may clasp your hands lightly in front of you, clasp them lightly behind you, or place them palms-together at your chest/heart level.

Whether walking clockwise or counterclockwise, place one foot forward, and begin your walk.

Take smaller steps than usual.

Move slower than usual.

Allow your shoulders to relax and your face to become softer, which often begins with releasing any tension in your jaw.

Remain aware of the ground beneath you, your body moving through space, your clothes moving on your body, and your breath.

Focus your eyes on the ground before you.

You may choose to sync your breathing with your steps. For example, exhale on every third step (or what feels right for you), then inhale, take three more steps, then exhale.

You may wish to have a starting and end point that represents one full revolution around the circle. But remember, in meditation there is no destination; rather, we arrive in each moment.

When the mind wanders, return to your breath, and to the connection of your feet on the ground.

Just like thoughts, feelings and emotions may arise. Be with them. Don't fight to suppress them, but also realize that they do not define you but rather are something you are experiencing in this moment. It often helps to simply label them for what they are: "This is confusion," "This is stress," "This is fear," "This is clarity," "This is peace."

As you walk, allow your body to continue to settle. You can mentally think of your stress, worries, concerns, etc., all slipping off your back—lightening your load as you walk the circle. You can picture yourself becoming lighter, or stronger, with each completed circle.

Also leave room for all this to disappear and simply be, just walking the circle with no manufactured intentions or searching awareness, but rather embracing the emptiness, and limitlessness, that the circle represents.

For variety, or when really feeling the need to get centered, you may wish to drop your attention down into your center, the space two inches below your navel in the center of you, and walk from this center point. (See the Centering Walk, page 165.)

Perform the Walking Meditation (Circle Style) for five to twenty minutes.

TAKEAWAYS AND REFLECTIONS

Did anything surprise you about the Walking Meditation (Circle Style)? Were you able to stay focused? Did you set an intention prior to engaging in your walk, or did you repeat an affirmation during your walk? If so, how did that feel?

Did you get to a point where thoughts left you, and you could simply be? Did you feel more centered and at peace?

Jot down or make mental notes of any takeaways and reflections you may have, and continue the Walking Meditation (Circle Style) when it calls to you or when new circle walking areas and opportunities present themselves.

Thank you for your wholeness. I appreciate your ability and desire to embrace all that you are.

WALK 13
Walking Meditation (Walking the Labyrinth)

*Labyrinths offer the opportunity to walk in meditation
to that place within us where the rational merges with
the intuitive and the spiritual is reborn.*

—HELEN CURRY, *The Way of the Labyrinth*

OVERVIEW

Are you familiar with labyrinths? Have you ever walked one? On the surface, a labyrinth resembles a more traditional maze, but there are no false turns or dead ends in a labyrinth; it is one circuitous path that leads to the center.

There is a long history of contemplative walking done in labyrinths. Walking the labyrinth is seen as a journey into our own center, and back out again into the world. Other than being mindful and present in your walk, and respectful to others and the labyrinth itself, there is no one "right way" to do it. But there are certainly great depths to explore.

When searching for a labyrinth to walk, you will discover everything: from those that are put together with mismatched rocks and stones (I've had some of my favorite labyrinth experiences in these), to those that are carved into the earth or woven into garden hedges, to the often-elegant, elaborate indoor or outdoor labyrinths found at churches, cathedrals, and other sacred, unifying sites worldwide.

Even though the pathway may wind in ways that don't immediately make sense to you, it will always lead you to the center—so trust the path. (This can also translate to an often-valuable life lesson.)

Creating a labyrinth can be a fun and rewarding project for you, your family, your friends, or your walking group. There are many books and websites that will guide you through the process.

Here is a link to a great resource, The Labyrinth Society: https://labyrinthsociety.org. They also link to the World-Wide Labyrinth Locator site: https://labyrinthlocator.com.

BENEFITS

- Centers you.
- Focuses you.
- Calms you.
- Often helps you feel connected to something that is beyond you, or deeply woven into you.
- Teaches you to trust the path.
- Helps you to release the old and to embrace, or draw to you, the new.
- Allows you to complete something.
- Connects you to your spirit, or that still quiet voice inside of you.

WHEN TO DO

- When in need of calming, focusing, or grounding.
- When desiring to go inward and connect with your spirit, or the still quiet voice within you.
- When ready to release someone or something.
- When ready to embrace someone or something.
- When entering a new chapter in your life.
- When wanting to honor another.
- When wanting to feel a connection to something larger than you.
- When wanting to complete a journey inward and back.
- When grieving the loss of a loved one or any other loss.
- Children tend to love participating in labyrinth walks. It can be fun, focusing, and mysterious for them. It also tends to spur their creativity.

HOW TO DO

Stand before the entrance to the labyrinth.

Can be done barefoot when the location or terrain is appropriate.

Turn off your cellphone, switch it to airplane mode, or leave it behind.

You can now set an intention of something you'd like to receive or release while embarking on your journey inward and back out, or you can say a prayer that fits with your spiritual tradition and speaks to what you feel is right for you or another you may be praying for in this moment.

You may also wish to repeat an affirmation silently or aloud as you walk the labyrinth. Some examples are: "Walking this labyrinth, I receive all I need to receive, and I release all I need to release," "As I walk this labyrinth, I am open to receive my highest good," or "I walk this labyrinth for the highest good of all."

And of course you may choose to remain silent and receptive.

Perform your GBS Pre-Walk Check-In.

You may choose to lightly clasp your hands in front of you, clasp them behind your back, place them in prayer position (palms together) at your heart/chest level, or simply allow them to hang naturally.

Take another calming, centering breath, then enter the labyrinth.

Walk in a mindful manner. Be aware of your feet as they leave and return to the ground.

Do your best not to cut corners or allow your feet to stray outside the designated path.

Stay connected to your breath. Breathing easily in … and out … in … and out.

Usually you are in a labyrinth by yourself, but on occasion you may partake with a group, or you may simply encounter others passing you on their return from the center, or you passing them on their way into the center. When passing or trailing another, be mindful of allowing them adequate space, and also remain centered and grounded in *your* space. You may wish to acknowledge your fellow labyrinth walkers with a nod or smile when appropriate, or you may wish to honor their passing with little or no recognition.

When you reach the center of the labyrinth, you may see offer-ings that have been left behind; they may be religious or spiritual in nature, or even a simple coin, a feather, or photos of loved ones. You may choose to leave something as well—an offering, a remembrance, a dedication, or a simple "thank you." It is also okay to leave nothing behind.

Be sure to take a moment in the center to close your eyes, breathe, reflect, and maybe speak a few words of gratitude.

Then begin your way out: slowly, mindfully.

Oftentimes, people feel lighter or freer on their way out due to what they may have gained, or left behind or released—be it emo-tional, mental, physical, or spiritual.

Exit the labyrinth. Take a moment in stillness.

TAKEAWAYS AND REFLECTIONS

How was your journey through the labyrinth? Have you walked a labyrinth before?

Did you find it calmed you? Centered you? Do you feel you received something? Did you let go of something? Did you feel con-nected, perhaps even momentarily, to something beyond you? Did you remain focused throughout? Are there other labyrinths you'd like to explore?

Jot down or make mental notes of your labyrinth experience(s), and visit a labyrinth whenever a concentrated inner journey, experi-enced while walking, calls to you.

Walk 14
Destination-Manifestation Walk

Imagination is everything. It is the preview of life's coming attractions.

—ALBERT EINSTEIN

OVERVIEW

Be it a job, a behavior, a habit, a relationship, or an ongoing condition, the majority of us would like to change something in our lives. The Destination-Manifestation Walk gives us yet another tool to assist in doing so.

As mentioned earlier, the mind is very powerful. And tying that power of pretending (or imagining and envisioning) into a physically aligned activity, such as walking, can have a deep and life-changing effect.

Whether you tend to believe in the law of attraction, or that we as humans can magnetize things to us, there is no doubt that our thoughts and beliefs influence our decisions and what we draw to ourselves. "Manifestation," as it applies to this walk, means: *When your focused thoughts materialize in the physical world.*

The Destination-Manifestation Walk encourages you to enter a mind-body space that sets off a chain reaction of chemicals in the body, allowing you to begin to see and *feel* change, and invite it fully into you.

In short, it is not a miracle, but it is a tool (in the form of a walk) that helps you to focus in on and obtain what is most needed or desired in your life.

I find this practice even more powerful than the conventional, stationary, creative visualization, because you have engaged the body.

BENEFITS

- Helps us—as individuals, couples, or a group—to greater align with something we would like to manifest in our lives: be it a job, a completed project, a noble behavior, a healthy habit, a rewarding relationship, or a more vibrant body.

- Prompts you to see deeper into your wants and needs and begins the process of inviting them into fruition.
- Helps you develop focus, concentration, and mental clarity.
- Helps you to gain courage, confidence, and belief in yourself; and for some, belief in a higher power.
- Allows you to (literally) take embodied action-steps toward what you want or need in your life.

WHEN TO DO

- When in need of change.
- When desiring to, or needing to, draw something to you or your group.
- When wanting to feel focused and empowered.
- When wanting to explore how you would (and will) move and feel in your body upon accomplishing a long- or short-term goal or project.
- When wanting to bolster your courage, confidence, or belief.
- When wanting to try on the next chapter of your life.

How often should you perform the Destination-Manifestation Walk?

There are many reasons one may have for undertaking this walk, and many desired outcomes. Therefore, there is no one-size-fits-all answer to this. We do know that grooving in new habits, beliefs, and behaviors often takes time. Try this walk for a few days in a row, and see how it feels. If time and life permit, try it for twenty-one days straight. And remember to stay open and receptive to spontaneous change and immediate manifestation. Perhaps the very first walk will bring you exactly what you need.

HOW TO DO

Pick a destination tied to a distance that you know you can reach; it can be as far as several miles or as close as fifty feet (or less if you're feeling weak). Then assign the completion of this walk (its destination) with something you want to reach or *manifest*. In other words, if you are trying to reach a new place of calm in life, or a job or relationship that may seem elusive, or the completion of a project, place it at the end of the walk (at your destination)—a landmark, be it a tree, a building, or a space directly related to where you want to be—and *walk directly toward it*.

Turn off your cellphone, switch it to airplane mode, or leave it behind.

Allow yourself to be open to receiving insights, answers, guidance, and pertinent information before, during, and after your Destination-Manifestation Walk. For those who align with prayer, you can speak a prayer asking to receive, through the process of this walk, what is for your highest good and the highest good of all.

Perform your GBS Pre-Walk Check-In.

Stand at your starting point, knowing very well where you will end up.

Begin your walk, heading as *directly* as you can toward your destination. (Granted, just as life has twists and turns, some you see coming and some you don't, so may this walk; but see it through, the whole time focused, envisioning reaching this destination-manifestation.)

When you do reach your destination, be it a tree, sign, building, or any other meaningful or compelling landmark, *touch it*—you have arrived! And by arriving, you have accomplished what you set out to accomplish; you have reached the new job, your completed project, your new relationship, etc.

Now soak in the feeling of what it feels like to have reached your desired destination-manifestation. Really let it wash through you, fully embracing this manifestation. Allow yourself to feel the excitement, contentment, or presence—and let your body chemistry feel this shift in you.

Once you have fully locked into the feeling of accomplishment—of reaching what you set out to reach and manifest—begin your return walk.

As you walk back, allow your body, and your entire being, to be alive and to vibrate in this new way. *Own it*.

Walk as if you *have* the job, the relationship, the healthy habit, the noble behavior, the completed project, or whatever else you have chosen to walk this distance for.

Fully embody it, allowing it to move through and infuse your every step.

Each object your eyes land upon, each sound that reaches your ears, and every bump in the sidewalk should be seen, heard, and felt as this new you would respond to them.

Recognize your breathing, knowing that even your breathing can change.

Return to your starting place knowing that a shift has indeed occurred, and that you are, at the very least, one step closer to what you wish to manifest.

TAKEAWAYS AND REFLECTIONS

What was your Destination-Manifestation Walk like for you? Were you clear on what you wanted to manifest? What did it feel like when you reached your destination? Were you able to come more "alive" during your Destination-Manifestation Walk? Could you feel your body, your energy, and your mental outlook as it would feel upon accomplishing your specific manifestation?

Did anything surprise you? Scare you? Did clarity arrive—perhaps even a next action step to take?

Do you feel it would benefit you to repeat this specific walk, further aligning with your desired want or need, or do you now feel aligned with what you set out to manifest?

Jot down or make mental notes of your experience, and continue to revisit the Destination-Manifestation Walk whenever the call for change—both internal and external—arises.

WALK 15
Earth Below, Heavens Above Walk

If the stars should appear but one night every thousand
years how man would marvel and stare.

—RALPH WALDO EMERSON

OVERVIEW

When walking beneath the stars at night, I often think of the quote from Carl Sagan: "We are all made of star stuff." Chris Impey, professor of astronomy at the University of Arizona, further explains this as follows:

His [Sagan's] statement sums up the fact that the carbon, nitrogen and oxygen atoms in our bodies, as well as atoms of all other heavy elements, were created in previous generations of stars over 4.5 billion years ago. Because humans and every other animal as well as most of the matter on Earth contain these elements, we are literally made of star stuff.

We're made of star stuff. Maybe that's why, just as when we're in the presence of bodies of water, we feel a connection, we also feel something deep and indescribable within us when gazing up into the stars. Of course, the makeup of our human body aside, it is the sheer awe factor that often carries us into the starry realms, causing us to be transfixed.

On January 17, 1994, a 6.7 magnitude earthquake struck Los Angeles. At the time it struck, 4:31 a.m., I was asleep on the fifth floor of an older apartment building in Hollywood. As the walls shook and items began to fall, I made sure my girlfriend was okay, and waited until the shaking stopped, then we hopped up, grabbed what we could, including our dog, and made our way down the stairs and out onto the street.

The sirens began. And the damage made itself known. Los Angeles was indeed shaken.

But my biggest takeaway, besides witnessing people's desire to care for others and help one another, was looking up and seeing *a night sky full of stars*. It was literally out of this world. This was all due to the fact that much of the power in Los Angeles had gone out.

So there we were, a group of forty or so people, clumped together in the street, staring up in complete awe. There were stories of people calling 911 alarmed by what they saw in the sky: the *Milky Way*. With only a waxing crescent moon, the January 17 early morning sky was perfect.

Having experienced this and many other starry encounters, one of my wishes is that all people could see the night sky in its full, star-filled glory—and that it be not so foreign an occurrence to them that they call 911, nervous about an alien invasion.

Remember, there are more stars in the sky than there are grains of sand on all the beaches of the earth. We are on a little blue dot (earth) spinning on our axis at 1,000 miles per hour and orbiting our sun at an average speed of 67,000 miles per hour—all the while staring out into infinity.

Walking between dusk and dawn, with your head to the sky, can be like entering another world.

I encourage you to take the journey, even if it's just one shining star or a sliver of moon that reveals itself. Or maybe even a shooting star—just for you.

BENEFITS

- The heavens above will inspire you.
- Stimulate you.
- Connect you into a larger part of you.
- Encourage you to dream and see beyond life as you know it.
- Kids tend to love walking under the stars, especially when we let them dream. Be sure to tell them that there are more stars in the sky than there are grains of sand on all the beaches of the earth.

WHEN TO DO

- I know for many of you, based on location, an everyday view of the star-filled sky is not a reality. But whenever you can, and as often as possible, put yourself in a position to check in with the planets and stars.

- Whenever you are in a location with low light pollution, seek out the night sky.

- Best viewing occurs when the nights are longer, so autumn through spring—and during the days immediately before, after, or during the new moon. (The sun's reflection off the full moon produces its own light pollution; see Full Moon Walk, page 120.)

- Look to the night sky when in need of inspiration.

- When desiring a larger view of life.

- When wishing to remember your place in the cosmos.

- During a meteor shower, such as the Perseids meteor shower, which occurs every summer in the Northern Hemisphere.

- When needing to feel as if there's more to life than the challenges that face you, or the latest must-have product, or the often-confusing ways of our world.

HOW TO DO

Dress appropriately for this nighttime walk. Carry a flashlight if you'd like.

Walk in an area, be it a field, a beach, an open parking lot, an empty roadway, or a forest path, where you feel safe walking with your attention often directed upward.

Turn off your cellphone, switch it to airplane mode, or leave it behind. (Or, if so desired, leave it on and use one of the many star-identifying apps to tell you what you are viewing. Just turn on the app, point your cellphone at the sky, and the app will identify which planets or stars are in view.)

Perform your GBS Pre-Walk Check-In.

Begin walking.

As you walk, allow yourself to be drawn into the heavens above, but remain aware of your feet feeling a deep connection to the earth below.

If you're familiar with astronomy, feel free to search for and identify the stars and planets above you.

Take time to contemplate the bigger questions you may hold—or just the sheer magnificence of life itself.

Think about what the heavens above and the earth below can tell you, or inspire within you.

Breathe. Count the stars. Open to possibilities. Open to change. Open to greater understanding.

If it feels right, take time to settle into a larger, more expansive identity, and consider yourself as being part of the stars.

Allow your eyes to soften at times, taking in the heavens above and your earthly surroundings with a relaxed, yet expansive, gaze. (Visit the Soft Gaze Walk on page 191.)

Conclude your walk knowing that even when they cannot be seen, the stars above are always there shining for you.

TAKEAWAYS AND REFLECTIONS

What was it like for you to take your star stuff for a walk? Were you able to find a location with low light pollution? Were you already a stargazer, or someone who pays attention to the night sky?

Were you inspired? Did you feel a connection to the stars? Was there one particular star or planet you were drawn to? Could you glimpse the Milky Way?

Did you embark on this walk alone or with others?

Did you receive any insights?

Jot down or make mental notes of any takeaways and reflections you may have. And continue to walk under the stars every chance you get.

Walk 16
Full Moon Walk

You cannot look up at the night sky on the Planet Earth and not wonder what it's like to be up there amongst the stars. And I always look up at the moon and see it as the single most romantic place within the cosmos.

—TOM HANKS

OVERVIEW

There is perhaps no one thing so immediately captivating as catching an unexpected glimpse of a blazing full moon as it suddenly appears to us through the trees or buildings or above the roof or city or mountaintop.

For some of us, the full moon is a common sight, one we look for; but for the majority of us, it is not a sight we search for—and I believe that's why when the moon springs itself on us in a surprising moment, it often takes our breath away, or at least makes us say, "Wow, look at that."

This walk is about just that: looking at the full moon, as well as the world around us, as we walk beneath it.

Organized Full Moon Walks are offered in various places throughout most developed areas. You may wish to join in on one, or perhaps start your own.

BENEFITS

- Allows you to view, contemplate, and explore places and spaces you enjoy in the daylight—now awash in the illuminating glow of a full moon.

- Allows you to connect more deeply with our closest celestial neighbor.

- Allows you to feel inspired.

- Grows your perspective.

- Reminds you of the continual cycles of change, and the ebb and flow of life.

- Children tend to love Full Moon Walks, especially when you engage their imagination and also point out things to them—like the moon does *not* actually emit its own light but rather is reflecting the sun's light.

WHEN TO DO

- When wanting to experience common or familiar places that you enjoy in the daylight (or new places)—now under the glow of a full moon.

- When wanting to be inspired.

- When wanting to connect deeper to earth's closest celestial neighbor.

- When wanting to experience the full moon with your friends, family, walking group, or significant other.

- When wanting to grow your earthly perspective.

Specific "When to Do's"

- The full moon occurs roughly once every month, and even though I used the word "blazing" above to describe its luminosity, in reality, the moon has no light of its own; but rather its glow occurs when the earth is located directly between the sun and the moon, and the nearside of the moon is completely sunlit.

- Full moons are most noticeable on clear nights when there is an absence of cloud cover, but even when it's cloudy, the moon can be fun to walk under—watching and searching as the moon pops in and out between cloud breaks. (This is a great time to walk with kids, asking them to "find the moon" for you.)

- During a "supermoon," when the moon is closer to the earth than usual.

- During a "harvest moon," occurring close to the autumn equinox (most often September 22 or 23 in the Northern Hemisphere) and known to be orange in color due to its close proximity to the horizon.

HOW TO DO

Find out when the next full moon will occur. A quick internet search will provide this information.

Choose a place, be it near or far from home, where you feel comfortable and would like to walk and explore during the full moon. Beaches, parks, mountain areas, and paths and walkways near the ocean and sea can be ideal, but Full Moon Walks in a city can be equally as rewarding.

Dress appropriately for this nighttime walk. Carry a flashlight if you'd like. Feel free to carry binoculars to give you a closer look at the moon, including its interesting markings and its thousand-mile-wide craters.

Once at your starting point, turn off your cellphone, switch it to airplane mode, or leave it behind.

Perform your GBS Pre-Walk Check-In.

With your feet remaining in connection to the earth, begin your walk as a group, with family, or solo.

Look at familiar or new objects and surroundings in the light of the full moon.

Look at trees, buildings, cars, water, leaves, shapes, animals, and people, all in the moonlight.

Look at the moon itself from various vantage points. Track it as you walk.

Notice shadows: your own and others'.

Listen. Breathe. Open to possibilities. Open to change. Open to illumination, understanding, and greater perspectives. Allow your eyes to soften at times, taking in the moon and your surroundings with a relaxed, yet expansive, gaze. (Visit the Soft Gaze Walk on page 191.)

Feel your body and the all of you as you walk on earth under the light of the sun reflecting off the moon, realizing that what you are experiencing, and what you yourself are a part of, is nothing short of amazing.

Wave your farewell to the Man in the Moon, and conclude your walk.

TAKEAWAYS AND REFLECTIONS

What was your Full Moon Walk like? Were you inspired? Have you participated in Full Moon Walks before? Were you able to appreciate things, spaces, and places (including the moon) that you may not have appreciated before? Did you feel larger, or perhaps smaller, than you normally do? What did you learn about yourself and your surroundings from your Full Moon Walk?

Jot down or make mental notes of your experiences, and keep your eyes open for the next full moon. It may just be a bright orange harvest moon.

WALK 17
Mindfully Walking Your Dog Walk

Dog is a man's best friend.

—attributed to King Frederick II of Prussia

OVERVIEW

If a dog is man's best friend, then walking with a dog must be pretty special.

The truth is I know many people who only walk—except for getting from point A to point B—when taking their dog(s) for a walk. This is not a sad reality. It's simply *a* reality. And there's a lot of good here. It gets them out, they spend time with their friend(s), and they get to have a routine.

Seeing how much dogs bring to our lives, including boundless unconditional love, many people would agree that a dog is man's best friend. With that said, it is my hope that the following walk will add to the list of gifts your dog brings to you—and perhaps it will be a gift for your dog as well.

For the professional dog walkers out there, this can be a challenging and fun, and potentially overwhelming, experience for you. But what a treat you will have by learning from each of your dogs, or packs of dogs.

Walking your dog can at times feel like a chore, maybe even boring or stressful, and at other times pure joy. The Mindfully Walking Your Dog Walk can turn this ordinary routine into a walk that grows your awareness of not only yourself, but also your canine friend, and how you relate as one, and to the world around you.

Does your dog listen to you? Do you listen to and feel your connection with your dog?

As a longtime walker, often with dogs, I've seen enough to know there is much to glean from this human/canine walking relationship. Since you're already doing it, why not learn what you can from it?

A quick story: Years ago while living in Los Angeles, I had a dog that I would take on pretty much the same walk every day. It was a responsibility, but also something I enjoyed. Then I started to notice that my patience was becoming shorter with him, and that something had shifted in our everyday walk. What that something was, was stress. I had taken on a great deal and was under a lot of pressure, and the only way I came to realize this was through noticing this change while engaged in this one, familiar everyday activity. That's how it revealed itself. My dog wasn't doing anything different. There were no changes in the neighborhood. The changes were within me. I was grateful to be shown this, and I began to gauge my stress level by how I was feeling and responding while walking my dog.

Since we're exploring mindful and guided walking on our own or with other humans, it's a good time to extend that practice to include this animal friend at your side or at the end of its leash. And when your human friends ask you if you meditate, say, "Yeah, I meditate with my dog."

BENEFITS

- Grows your bond with your dog.
- Expands your awareness.
- Helps you learn more about yourself and your environment.
- Uncovers habits and patterns that may be unproductive or harmful to you and/or your dog.
- Allows you to plug mindfulness meditation into a familiar daily activity.
- Encourages you to read this book to your dog and have him or her post a stellar review on Amazon.

WHEN TO DO

- When you want to discover habits and patterns that may or may not be serving you and/or your dog well.

- When you want to really tune into and be present to your animal companion.

- When you want to use mindfulness to turn the ordinary into the extraordinary—or at least something far more interesting.

- When wanting to learn more about yourself and your environment.

HOW TO DO

Settle on a day and time when you can walk your dog without having to rush. In other words, the act of walking with your dog is the priority, not the act of completing the walk.

Turn off your cellphone, switch it to airplane mode, or leave it behind.

Perform your GBS Pre-Walk Check-In.

Prepare for your walk as you normally do. But from the very beginning, become *aware* of each step in the process—and the walk.

If you use a leash/lead, begin by being present while retrieving it from its stored location.

Feel yourself reaching or bending for it. Consider the place you keep it. Which hand do you grab it with? How does it feel in your hand? Notice its weight, its texture, its color, perhaps even its smell.

When it's in your hand, note how you feel, and how your dog feels.

Be present and focused as you attach it to your dog. Slow down enough to notice the ring on your dog's collar that it attaches to, or the harness it may attach to. Notice the color of the collar or harness.

See how you feel now that you and your dog are connected in this manner.

Are you still grounded? How is your breathing?

Remain present to your breath, to the ground beneath you, and to the space around you.

Listen to your voice: the level, the sound, and any inflections you use.

With all your senses engaged, begin your walk.

Whatever pace you end up walking, feel each foot as it rises, touches down, and rises again.

Feel when you are in your center and when you're pulled out of your center—granted, a large dog can often pull you off your physical center, but can you stay emotionally and mentally centered? (You may wish to experiment with walking your dog from your center point; see the Centering Walk, page 165.)

Remember, this walk is about noticing, not fixing (any fixing would come later).

Is the leash a good fit for you and your dog? Do you feel it's a good weight and length?

Are your shoes comfortable?

How's the temperature today?

Look at what your dog looks at.

Try to keep your muscles relaxed (including your jaw) as you lead, and at times are led by, your dog.

Notice your breathing. Then notice your dog's breathing.

Notice where your attention goes when you are walking together, also when the dog pauses to sniff, mark its territory, or relieve itself. Continue to be in this walk, and nowhere else.

Notice or discover something new: A tree. A sign. A scent. Someone's car. The sound of your footsteps. The sound of your dog's steps. A sound you may not have heard or paid attention to before.

Become aware of who you are, or at least who you are in this moment, as you walk your dog.

As you conclude your walk, go through the same "awake and present" process of reentering your house or car or other starting point, and being mindfully aware as you bend or reach to remove your dog's leash, then return it to its place of storage. Then check in with yourself. Once again feel your feet on the ground, be aware of your breath in your body, and sense the space around you.

You just meditated with your dog.

TAKEAWAYS AND REFLECTIONS

What did you learn from the Mindfully Walking Your Dog Walk? Did you notice anything right from the beginning? Perhaps when you first picked up the leash? Was it easy for you to be fully present throughout the walk? Was it difficult?

If you are used to engaging with your cellphone while walking your dog, was it difficult not to? Did it feel like a beneficial break?

Did you notice anything in your environment that you had not noticed before?

What did you learn about your physical body? Did you pick up on any habits that may not be serving you and/or your dog well? How was your breathing? Were you able to stay centered, to in a sense "hold your ground," or were you pulled off your physical and mental center?

Do you think your dog noticed the difference in you during this walk?

Do you feel there is a way to bring more ease into the walk?

Jot down or make mental notes of all you experienced during this time with your animal friend, and continue to consider your takeaways and reflections as you further grow your practice of mindfully walking your dog.

WALK 18
Forgiving Others Walk

To forgive is to set a prisoner free and discover that the prisoner was you.

—LEWIS B. SMEDES

OVERVIEW

Forgiveness. Perhaps the hardest thing to give, yet also the most powerful.

Why is it powerful? Because it frees you. How does it free you? By bringing you out of the past, where your pain, hurt, shame, uncertainty, and any sense of betrayal exist, and into the present. Why does this matter? It matters because in the present, *you* have the choices (and the power), not others.

People may have harmed you. They may have done so knowingly or unknowingly. They may be aware of the pain or discomfort or inconvenience they caused you, or they may be unaware. They may wish to be forgiven, or they may not wish to be forgiven. They may think of you every day, or they may not think of you at all. All this is on them.

What is on you, is to heal, thrive, and become whole again. This begins by uprooting what is living in you, feeding on you, pulling you down in large or small ways, and continually fueled by your holding on.

There are hundreds of inspiring, tearjerker videos where we see people confronting and forgiving others. These videos often go viral, and I believe they do so because we can all relate—or we all *want* to relate. Along with this, I feel these videos speak to the inherent goodness and love in each of us—a love that we all wish to share and experience.

Forgiveness is a process, and the initial act of forgiving begins with the desire (or the now felt need) to do so. It does not have to be a singular person that you are to forgive now; it could be your family, your entire high school class, twenty kids from summer camp who made life miserable for you, or whoever or whatever else.

Embracing and engaging in this walk will get the wheels of forgiveness turning. The walk may stir up feelings, issues, and discomforts that you may have been stuffing down. You may feel a wave of wide-ranging emotions, including feeling great. Be prepared for any and all.

This walk is for you. It is placed here to assist you in forgiving another. It is part of your moving forward (starting literally with footsteps) and returning home to wholeness.

BENEFITS

- Allows you to get closure on something that you may have kept open and carried within you for a long time.
- Allows you to feel lighter.
- Welcomes you into the present in a way that will lead to a healthier future.
- Reduces stress, and can lower blood pressure.
- Opens up your breathing.
- Can improve your heart health.
- Helps the forgiven to heal.
- Makes the world an even brighter place.

WHEN TO DO

- When it's time. The fact that you're reading this may tell you the time is now.
- When you can be alone with yourself.
- When you have ten or more minutes to just be.
- When and where you feel safe, comfortable, and perhaps even inspired.
- Repeat the Forgiving Others Walk as needed.

HOW TO DO

Find a time when you can be on your own, undisturbed.

Find a place to walk where you feel comfortable, perhaps even inspired.

Consider who or what you are now ready to forgive, while also remaining open to what may emerge while walking.

You may wish to carry a notebook and a pen in case you feel moved to jot anything down.

You may wish to bring tissues or a handkerchief.

Turn off your cellphone, switch it to airplane mode, or leave it behind.

Settle into your GBS Pre-Walk Check-In.

You may wish to set an intention as to what you will receive via this walk. For example, "I walk this walk in forgiveness, now ready and willing to release what no longer serves me and my highest good." If prayer aligns for you, you may also wish to speak a prayer, asking to open yourself to forgiving, and to be given the strength, clarity, and understanding to do so.

Nothing about this walk is to make life harder for you. Even the walk itself can be easier than you even think to be effective. It is 100 percent done at your pace, be it a meandering stroll or a fast-footed jaunt, or anything in between. Remember, this is not about exercise, but rather is an exercise in forgiveness, and it will be done at your own pace and in your own way.

Begin your walk.

As you walk, know that you are a sovereign being, and that you— and only you—are the deciding factor in your strength, happiness, joy, and understanding. (You may wish to even affirm this aloud to yourself: "I am a sovereign being, and I and only I am responsible for my happiness, joy, strength, and understanding.")

Settle into a pace that feels right to you.

Remain connected to your breath; and as you walk, say either silently or aloud: "I forgive." Say this a number of times, in sync with your outbreath: on every exhale, "I forgive." Keep only these two words in your mind and your heart as you walk. They will become your mantra for this walk.

When you become comfortable saying these words, you can address the message to whomever or whatever you wish to forgive. As you exhale, say, "I forgive [so-and-so or such-and-such]."

You do not have to fill in the story or replay any moments (unless you desire to). You just have to say, "I forgive," along with who or what you are forgiving.

If it is a name or names that you find hard or discomforting to say aloud, then simply say, "I forgive you," or "I forgive them," or "I forgive all." Whatever works.

As you say this, know that on some level, they are receiving it. But even more importantly, in this moment, you are feeling it and receiving it. You are lightening yourself. You are allowing for a deep ease of breath to return to you. You are inviting in freedom: yours … and theirs.

You can speak this sentence of forgiveness as much as you'd like as you walk, and you can say it in any way you'd like: it may build into—and then through—anger, or you may find yourself getting to a point of unexpected laughter. Whatever the case, this is your walk, your way, at your time.

Also, you may find yourself walking differently: perhaps a feeling of buoyancy arrives, or clearer direction, or simply a sense that a shift has occurred within and around you, permitting you to move in a much freer sense.

As you return home or to wherever else you began your Forgiving Others Walk, know that you are now a different person. You invite in a new future, from a place of this newborn now.

TAKEAWAYS AND REFLECTIONS

Thank you for allowing yourself this walk. Thank you for your bravery in offering forgiveness. Thank you for exploring more deeply what it means to be human.

Reflect on what the experience of a Forgiving Others Walk was like for you, and what takeaways you may carry with you into the future.

Permit yourself to take any present-moment action-steps you feel called to take, including reaching out to whom you've forgiven. And always remember, forgiveness is a strength, not a weakness.

Walk 19
Forgiving Yourself Walk

Love yourself—accept yourself—forgive yourself—and be good to yourself, because without you the rest of us are without a source of many wonderful things.

—LEO BUSCAGLIA

OVERVIEW

What's often harder than forgiving others? Forgiving ourselves. Perhaps it's because we are often taught from a young age to forgive others, yet rarely are we taught that there will be times when we must also forgive ourselves, and that it's okay to do so.

I cannot count the number of times that I have encountered someone who is carrying something with them that they cannot (or will not) forgive themselves for. More often than not, it's a relatively small matter: something that was not handled well by them, or something that slipped by them, or something they were ill-equipped to handle in the first place. And of course, there are times when they've actually done nothing wrong at all. Whatever the case, they're carrying the weight, and it's not getting lighter.

Then slowly, with time and/or assistance, they allow themselves the same forgiveness, compassion, and understanding that they give to others. As this occurs, and as forgiveness takes root, they begin to change. They become lighter, clearer, healthier, more loving and accepting of themselves, and often more productive in their pursuits.

This walk is about self-forgiveness. As we know, forgiving ourselves is often a process, and it can certainly be more complex than a walk. But steps toward self-forgiveness, and the reflections, inquiry, and understanding they bring, are always steps in the right direction.

BENEFITS

- Sets you free.
- Can reduce anxiety and depression.
- Improves your immune function.
- Reconnects you to your joy.
- Opens your heart.
- Grows your self-worth.
- Makes others happy that you have (perhaps finally) forgiven yourself.
- Allows you to feel your lighter self.

WHEN TO DO

- When it's time to be free again.
- When you realize that holding onto your guilt or shame no longer serves you.
- When wanting to move forward in your life.
- When wanting to be an example (a light) to others.
- When knowing that you're worthy of your love, and so is the rest of the world.
- When enough has truly become enough.
- When wanting to set the other person (or people or whatever) free by freeing and forgiving yourself.

HOW TO DO

The first thing to know about how to do this walk is that it is your walk to do. Even though practices and prompts will be shared, you must also feel free to honor what arises in you. For instance, you may choose to sit at times, to hold onto something for support, to write something down for yourself or another, to turn back, or even to break into a freeing run. Any and all of this is fine, and may very well be part of your process.

Consider a place where you would like to walk.

Decide on a time when you can be on your own, undisturbed. (Of course you can also do this walk with a supportive walking partner.)

When possible, put on clothes that make you feel good.

Drink adequate water before heading out.

Consider again why it is now time to forgive yourself.

You may wish to carry a notebook and a pen in case you feel moved to jot anything down.

You may wish to bring tissues or a handkerchief.

Turn off your cellphone, switch it to airplane mode, or leave it behind.

Settle into your GBS Pre-Walk Check-In.

Allow yourself to breathe normally now. Remember, breath is life, breath is freedom, and breath is *now*.

You may wish to set an intention as to what you will receive via this walk. For example, "I walk this walk in forgiveness of myself; it is now time" or "Through this walk, I invite self-forgiveness into every fiber of my being." If prayer aligns for you, you may also wish to speak a prayer, asking that divine grace assist you in forgiving yourself.

Begin your walk in the direction and at the pace that feels most comfortable.

For the beginning of this walk, whether silent or aloud, settle into these words: "I am loved, and I am love." Even if this does not feel right to you, stay with it.

Breathe into this idea: "I am loved, and I am love."

This is all you have to focus on. Nothing else.

Hear it in your head, receive it into your heart, and at least a few times, hear yourself voicing it aloud.

When the time feels right (perhaps when you reach a certain land-mark or destination, or the words naturally occur or are ready to be pulled out by you), simply say, at whatever volume you can: "I forgive myself." You may also choose to say in detail what it is you are forgiving yourself for.

Allow yourself to feel what you need to feel, including any tension around these words. Just notice it. Simply be aware.

And now allow yourself to soften in any areas throughout your body that may be tensing or gripping.

Remain aware of any remorse that arises, and allow empathy for yourself, but also for others who may be connected to your past actions. Make yourself available to any intuitive wisdom you may need to hear, and to what, if anything, you may need to learn.

You may not need to say the words again: "I forgive myself." Only you will know.

But say them as often as you'd like, and at whatever volume feels right.

Let out some strong exhales. Swing your arms if you need to. Shake your body. Yell if it feels right and when the location is appropriate. Let your feet land solidly on the ground, feeling its support as you continue walking in forgiveness.

You may find yourself walking differently: perhaps a feeling of buoyancy arrives, or clearer direction, or simply a sense that a shift has occurred within and around you, permitting you to move in a much freer way.

Explore this as you take in the world around you.

As you conclude your walk, tell yourself: "I have entered a new chapter. I walk free of my past. I am forgiven."

TAKEAWAYS AND REFLECTIONS

Thank you for taking the steps in forgiving yourself.

How are you feeling after your Forgiving Yourself Walk? Did you encounter any barriers to self-forgiveness? Did anything arise that caught you off guard? Did you feel, "Yes, the time is now"? Did you release the weight—or at least part of it? Did you learn something about yourself and your past actions? Are there any action steps that you now feel the need to take? Did you feel empathy toward others as you forgave yourself?

As stated earlier, forgiveness—especially self-forgiveness—is a process, so be on the lookout for triggers that may conjure threads of old beliefs about yourself in regard to this action.

WALK 20
Dedication Walk

Act as if what you do makes a difference. It does.

—WILLIAM JAMES

OVERVIEW

Some of the most beautiful and memorable places, speeches, songs, books, and other items and creative endeavors have been born, or preserved, from the idea of a dedication to another, or to many.

In its own quiet way, this walk will add to a long list of memorable dedications, many of which, whether you know it or not, have touched and even shaped your life.

You may wish to dedicate a walk to someone who has recently passed or someone who was recently born; to a dear friend or someone who has positively impacted your life; to someone you used to walk with, or someone who can no longer walk; or even to an endeavor or an idea, such as kindness or beauty; or, finally, to nature, God, or life itself.

Perform the Dedication Walk as an individual, a family, or a group, all in alignment with a specific dedication.

In this spirit, I dedicate this walk to you.

BENEFITS

- Allows you to focus on another, be it a single person, an organization, or even an idea.

- Shows your love, presence, and appreciation for someone or something apart from you, but connected to you.

- Allows you to align your energy/energies in the service or honoring of another.

- Lifts your spirits.

WHEN TO DO

- When you want to honor another person, place, project, or idea, through the physical act of walking.

- When a location reminds you of another or calls to you in a significant way.

- When you wish to allow another to see a part of the world through your eyes.

- When it feels like the right thing to do.

- On someone's birthday or other landmark moment in time, such as Memorial Day or Earth Day.

HOW TO DO

Whether on your own or as a group, decide what or who you wish to walk in dedication of.

Decide on the perfect walking spot and time. (Note: Sometimes the spot and time pick you.)

Prior to walking, perform your GBS Pre-Walk Check-In, allowing yourself to become fully present.

You may wish to carry or wear something in honor of the person, persons, or whatever you are walking in dedication of.

You may wish to share stories about the person, persons, or whatever you are walking in dedication of.

You may wish to sing songs in honor of and in dedication to the person, persons, or whatever you are walking in dedication of.

You may wish to make the entire walk a silent walk.

As you walk, allow yourself to carry the essence of the person, project, or idea with you as an individual or as a group.

Embody what or who it is you are walking in dedication of. Take your steps in embodied dedication.

You may choose a walk with a beginning or an end destination that speaks to the dedication, such as a lake, a waterfall, a building, or a home that has significance; a town, a park, a tree, or other meaningful landmarks or areas.

You may choose to *call in* your official dedication when reaching this destination, or it can be part of the entire walk. And of course you can set a plaque or whatever else aligns with your dedication.

Conclude your Dedication Walk in a manner that seems most fitting.

TAKEAWAYS AND REFLECTIONS

Thank you for taking a Dedication Walk. I find it quite beautiful to walk in dedication.

If it feels right, jot down or make mental notes of some of your takeaways and reflections, including what you may have learned and experienced from your Dedication Walk.

But mostly, know that what you did is powerful, effective, and appreciated. In your own large or small way, you have added to the many impactful dedications offered throughout our world.

WALK 21
Prayer Walk

My walking is first of all a prayer for peace. If you give your life as a prayer, you intensify prayer beyond all measure.

—PEACE PILGRIM

OVERVIEW

The standard definitions of prayer, according to the *Oxford Dictionary*, are: "a solemn request for help or expression of thanks addressed to God or an object of worship" and "an earnest hope or wish." Here, the prayer may be the walk itself.

There are many who do not believe in a God or a higher organizing intelligence, and therefore do not resonate with the conventional act of prayer in the religious sense. You yourself may fall into this category. Please do not let that dissuade you from seeing if there is anything of value for you in the Prayer Walk.

It is not a walk to convert another, although for some it may serve as such, but rather a walk to speak to—or into—something larger than us. It is a walk to invite the divine or sacred, or "all that is good," into our minds, into our hearts, and right down to our feet and into the very earth we exist on, in a way that elevates us yet grounds us as we seek to be a vessel of goodness and to share our highest expression—and focused care—in the service of all.

Peace Pilgrim, formerly known as Mildred Norman, walked more than 25,000 miles across the United States spreading her message: "This is the way of peace: Overcome evil with good, falsehood with truth, and hatred with love." This was her walking prayer, and she lived it for twenty-eight years, from 1953 to 1981.

And of course there have been prayer walks and pilgrimages for centuries.

More and more, our technology-driven world is creating less space within the home for quiet, contemplative prayer. That makes the practice of a Prayer Walk all the more valuable.

For me personally, I find prayer, whether it be stationary or moving, to be very comforting, illuminating, healing, and effective. Comforting, because it allows me to feel as if there is something larger that we are connected to that is working with us, even when it does not always appear that way. Illuminating and healing, because I have found that often the unexplainable is revealed and made manifest through prayer, including healings. Effective, because I believe the act of prayer directs our energy into certain areas of life, be it a person, a situation, or a problem, that through whatever occurrence, causes change. Having said this, the mystery of God, life, and prayer is much bigger than any of us will ever truly understand, including those who have dedicated their life to prayer.

May this walk align you with, or strengthen, your own sense of prayerful connection.

BENEFITS

- Plugs you into something greater than you, yet also something you are very much a part of.

- Further aligns you with your spirit, or higher consciousness, or what some refer to as the higher self, and that still quiet voice within you.

- Allows you to be of service to "the whole," even while focusing on one aspect of the whole.

- Opens you to further inspiration, answers, and understanding.

- Allows you to focus your prayer at or on a specific location.

- Opens your heart.

- Allows you to physically exercise your body as you pray on behalf of yourself or another person, persons, institutions, ideas, or principles (such as Peace Pilgrim walking for peace).

- Can lead to inner transformation.

- In this modern age of constant distractions within the home, a prayer walk can help you remain present and focused on your prayer.

WHEN TO DO

- When wanting to enter into prayer on behalf of a person, place, thing, or idea.
- When led by a deep inner calling.
- When seeking prayerful union with the divine.
- When wanting to walk in honor of something larger than you.
- When feeling directionless, confused, or uninspired.
- When wanting to be of service.
- At the beginning or end of your day.
- When needing to be alone with your prayers.

HOW TO DO

Pick your location, whether it be right outside your living space or another location that either inspires you in a contemplative, prayerful way, or where you feel called to walk in prayer.

You may wish to walk alone, with a prayer partner, with a group, or with family members.

You may clearly know for what reason you are embarking on a prayer walk—to whom or what you are offering your prayer—or you may need to more deeply inquire within yourself, ask those close to you, or ask God or a higher intelligence for inspiration.

You may wish to pray for a specific person, neighborhood, community, or virtue, or you may wish to pray for everything and everyone you pass. You may wish to carry a prayer list, with names of people or themes you'd like to pray for while walking. Or you may wish to engage in a conversation with the divine, or simply express your love and awe for life, or recite your favorite prayer, verse, or poem.

It's also okay if it's a more secular prayer, where you simply offer "well wishes and hope" to all around you—or if you choose to walk in complete silence, to offer your walk as your prayer.

If you are unclear in your focus, pray for someone's well-being; for clarity of action; for greater understanding; for the deepening of your faith; for the reversal of your anger; and that your eyes be opened to what you need to see, your ears be opened to what you need to hear, and your heart be opened to all that needs to heal.

When your starting point is established, turn off your cellphone, switch it to airplane mode, or leave it behind.

Perform your GBS Pre-Walk Check-In. As you do, allow yourself to become centered and receptive, and to become aware of your breath, your feet on the ground, and the space around and above you. You may feel—while sensing the space within and around you—what may be described as a connection into *something larger*. Breathe with it.

Begin your walk knowing that there is no set or required distance for this walk, other than what you assign to it or feel inspired to do.

While engaged in your act of outward and inward prayer, remain open to moments of receptive silence, knowing that great wisdom is often born of silence. Remember, walking can put us in a very relaxed and receptive state.

Take in the sights, sounds, scents, and feelings that emerge; and allow for inspiration and guidance.

If and when you feel the need to close your eyes for some moments, do so. And if you feel the need or calling to pause, sit, or switch directions, do so.

Make yourself available to deeper understandings, and even answers to past prayers. Stay connected to the ground beneath you, the breath within you, and the space around you.

Conclude your walk, whether it be "to be continued" at another time or not, knowing that whatever your beliefs about prayer may be, the act of walking in service to, and love for, another, and creation itself, is quite a beautiful endeavor.

TAKEAWAYS AND REFLECTIONS

Thank you for walking in prayer, whatever your version of this may have been.

What was your Prayer Walk experience like? Did you find that you could be fully present? Did you feel in alignment with something greater than you, or perhaps with your heart?

I commend us all for taking time to ponder and further connect with the great mystery of our existence, and focus on the greater well-being of our fellow men and women and the planet.

Jot down or make mental notes of any insights, understandings, or feelings that may have emerged during your Prayer Walk. Know that the path of prayer, whether walked or spoken behind closed doors, will often rise to those who seek to meet it, and yield benefits both seen and unseen.

Lastly, my prayer is that we may honor a woman who dedicated her life to peace, walking more than 25,000 miles, and that we do so by living (and walking) her message, to "Overcome evil with good, falsehood with truth, and hatred with love."

WALK 22
Affirmation Walk

Affirmation statements are going beyond the reality of the present into the creation of the future through the words you use in the now.

—LOUISE HAY

OVERVIEW

Earlier I mentioned the power and effectiveness of positive affirmations not only in helping us to rewrite our negative self-talk, limiting or unkind beliefs, and subconscious patterns, but also as a way for us to discover these things.

Unlike the other walks where I suggest assigning or layering in an affirmation to further deepen or clarify your walk, the Affirmation Walk is 100 percent focused on your chosen affirmation.

Repeating an affirmation while walking allows you to flood your entire being with your chosen affirmation—to wear it and integrate it while you move. Walking also releases what science calls the "happiness hormones"—oxytocin, serotonin, dopamine, and endorphins—so as you're walking and affirming, you're also receiving an extra chemical boost to assist in your shift.

Science has told us that our thoughts and words are heard by every cell in our body. So when you walk, and you affirm silently or aloud to yourself—or out to the entire universe—know that, and envision, every cell in your body is not only hearing you, but being affected.

The Affirmation Walk is a walk of empowerment, of change, of drawing to you, and wiring into you, what will serve you best, and releasing from you what no longer serves you.

It is a way to further tune in, become aware, and transform.

BENEFITS

- Allows you to make positive changes at a very deep level.

- Opens you to new opportunities and ways of viewing yourself and the world.

- Helps you to see where you may be harming yourself, or others, or holding yourself back.

- Allows you to move and engage with your body in a way that is connected to a change or changes you would like to make.

- Elevates your self-esteem and allows you to more greatly love, respect, connect with, and grow yourself.

- Strengthens your faith.

- Helps you to heal.

WHEN TO DO

- When ready to feel better.

- When wanting to make a positive change in your thoughts and beliefs about yourself, your relationships, or other aspects of the world.

- When wanting to uncover and uproot old, limiting, and detrimental thoughts and beliefs, and replace them with more positive, beneficial ones.

- When wanting to release something, or draw something to you.

- When needing a break—and a breakthrough.

- When needing to affirm a position, outcome, or decision.

- When feeling anxious.

*How often and for how long
should you repeat your affirmations?*

Everyone and each situation is different. The simple answer is: until you start to see or feel a change taking place. This can at times happen quickly, such as elevating your mood, or giving you greater clarity; or it may take longer, for instance when seeking to create large-scale change in your life—or undo a deep-seated belief—or when your affirmation may be tied into others who are co-creating something with you, and the collective timing then becomes a factor. As a guideline, consider speaking each affirmation for twenty-one days.

Also, the Affirmation Walk does not have to be a special walk: something you set aside a time of day for. It is something you can integrate into any walk you do, like walking to your car or around town. The important thing is for you to be engaged in the process.

HOW TO DO

Choose a time when you can focus on you. Granted, you may not *have* the time to focus on you. This may be something you want to look deeper into—and begin to change through your Affirmation Walk, allowing time for your personal well-being: "I allow time for my personal well-being." And of course, you can also do this anytime you find yourself walking.

Choose a place where you would like to walk, or a familiar walking area that you feel comfortable in.

When possible, wear clothes that make you feel good and that represent you in your healthiest, most inspired or uplifted way. Wear comfortable footwear as well.

Choose a single affirmation to focus on for the duration of your walk. When selecting a positive affirmation, begin by working with what is currently occupying your thoughts and beliefs in a negative or detrimental way. For example, "I'll never find a job." Your affirmation can be as simple and direct as "I will find a job" or a more nuanced version, "The job I need is heading my way. I take the right steps to meet it." Or, as some people prefer, affirm it as if it has already happened: "I have a job."

You may also wish to turn your negative self-talk into positive affirmations. For example, if you frequently tell yourself, "I am unlovable" or "Life stinks," you can turn those phrases into affirmations that serve you: "I am lovable" and "Life is beautiful." Or even: "I openly accept love into all aspects of my life and being" and "I grow from life's challenges."

Some affirmations to consider and/or implement:

- "I love myself."
- "I am healthy."
- "I am safe."
- "I am valuable."
- "Life works."
- "Everything will be okay."
- "The answers and insights I need arrive at the perfect time."
- "I approve of myself."
- "I get stronger every day."
- "I look for and see the good in all people, including myself."
- "It's okay to rest."

For those with a religious or spiritual inclination, you can create and speak affirmations that align with, or are born of, your faith. Some examples are:

- "With God all things are possible."
- "I am one with all of life."

- "I am loved by God."
- "I can do all things through Christ who strengthens me."
- "Through my faith, all my needs shall be met."
- "I am spirit. And spirit is limitless."

Before you begin your walk, perhaps even the day or night before, allow yourself to look deep into yourself and your life and see what is either right on the surface or wired deeper into you that now needs to be uprooted, changed, or mentally upgraded.

Turn off your cellphone, switch it to airplane mode, or leave it behind.

Perform your GBS Pre-Walk Check-In. See what arises in your mind. It might be "This Affirmation Walk is a stupid idea. I'm going to watch TV instead." If a thought like this arises, simply thank it for presenting itself, and let it go, with the help of a strong exhale.

Begin your walk.

As you walk, whether it be fifty feet, a hundred yards, or multiple miles, repeat your chosen affirmation. You may do so quietly or with more outward strength. Either way, do so with conviction. It's beneficial to hear yourself say the words; it's also valuable to repeat them in your head—getting used to them, as you would a positive thought. Feel free to get creative; you can even create a song from your affirmation.

You can repeat your affirmation with the rhythm of your steps or your breath, or you can just let it flow naturally.

The key element is to let yourself *feel* it, even if it feels strange or foreign at first.

If something arises within you during your walk, and you feel moved to switch your affirmation, do so.

If and when negative self-talk arises or stray thoughts that are unproductive come, allow them to drift off, much like an overhead cloud, and return to your affirmation. If an emotion arises, be with it; don't force it down. Breathe. And if you need to pause, sit, or lie down, do so.

As you walk, allow for a positive shift to take place. Look for the good. See it. Discover it. Feel it. And let it see, discover, and feel you as well.

Remember, a lot of these long-held, negative, or limiting thoughts, beliefs, and ideas did not originate in or with you, but are societal, or were handed down or imposed upon you by people who just didn't know better or could not do better.

At the conclusion of your Affirmation Walk, take a moment to further settle into and reflect on what you have affirmed; and allow yourself to carry it forth in mind, body, and spirit throughout the rest of your waking day and into your sleep.

TAKEAWAYS AND REFLECTIONS

What did you learn from your Affirmation Walk? Are you new to positive affirmations? Have you perhaps done them before but haven't tied them to exercise or walking? Did focusing on an affirmation affect how you felt as you walked? Did you perhaps notice a shift taking place?

Remember, affirmations allow us to not only see who we are (or believe ourselves to be) but also who we can be.

Jot down or make mental notes of anything that may have arisen during your Affirmation Walk, and also know that change is a process that we must continue to show up for, and it can often be scary. But *do show up*, and know that you're more than worthy of all you've affirmed.

WALK 23
Gratitude Walk

Gratitude is the healthiest of all human emotions. The more you express gratitude for what you have, the more likely you will have even more to express gratitude for.

—ZIG ZIGLAR

OVERVIEW

In nearly every talk I've given, when asked what one thing someone could do to improve their life, my answer has been: *gratitude*. Cultivate an attitude of gratitude. And of course this goes way beyond my words and experiences; it seems as if it's nearly every week that science further confirms a positive health attribute, or finds a new one, linked to practicing or living in gratitude.

Just as forgiveness allows you to reclaim your wholeness, gratitude or "thankfulness" allows you to reclaim and grow your happiness. And just like forgiving, gratitude can be challenging; but I assure you that counting your blessings is a transformative practice that is well worth your investment.

A culture that does not teach us to be thankful for what we have, but rather that we will only be whole (and happy) when we have or attain more, leads to a never-ending must-have-more-to-be-more sickness that has infected so many of us.

Counting your blessings via a Gratitude Walk takes you down a very healthy road, one "thankful step" at a time.

You may choose to do this walk alone or with others. Joining forces to share what we are thankful for is very powerful. Whether you are walking with your best friend, your partner, your child, your walking group, or even a stranger, sharing in this way will allow for some beautiful, heart-opening, life-affirming, happiness-hormones-releasing interactions that will elevate the already positive act of walking into a happiness-compounding, nurturing, relationship-deepening, mind-body-spirit experience that will live on long after your group walk is completed.

BENEFITS

- Elevates your mood, increases happiness, and puts a smile on your face.

- Recenters and focuses you.

- Calms you.

- Helps you break free of toxic thoughts and emotions.

- Rewires your brain to look at things differently.

- Cultivates an appreciation for what may not have been appreciated before.

- Raises self-esteem and enhances empathy.

- Improves sleep.

- Opens you to inspiration.

- When performing this walk with others, it allows you—and perhaps your walking group or partner—to be heard, received, and appreciated.

- Shifts perspectives, deepens relationships, and cultivates a more positive outlook.

- Teaches you and your group or partner to appreciate what may have been previously overlooked.

WHEN TO DO

- When needing a mental, emotional, or spiritual lift.

- When needing to see beyond your current problems and struggles.

- When wanting to shift your mindset from negative to positive.

- When wanting to make changes for the better.

- When ready for inspiration.

- When needing to count your blessings.

- When wanting to share gratitude.

- When ready for positive change to occur.

HOW TO DO: ALONE

Choose a time and a place that are comfortable for you: a time when you won't have to rush, and a place where you can maybe even gather a sense of peace from the surroundings. Overall, it is great if you can dedicate twenty or more minutes to walking in gratitude; this will further ensure the release of happiness hormones and uplifting neurotransmitters.

This entire walk is about engaging expressions of gratitude, many from within you, and others from the outside world. Some you will have to search for, like the elusive name of a childhood friend; some will spill right out of you; some, like a beautiful sunset, will appear before your eyes; and some, as when you realize a hurt from the past has made you stronger in the present, may take a little massaging before they land fully as something you are thankful for.

With that said, there is no getting this walk "wrong." The very intent of walking in gratitude will benefit you.

For those who are challenged by gratitude, realize that gratitude is a muscle that, like all muscles, gets stronger, and becomes more familiar to you, through repetition.

There are two main ways to perform this walk. The first is engaging the walk at a pace that is continually moving, and *tying your expressions of gratitude into your steps*. The second is a slower, stop-and-go, more contemplative practice; for this practice, you may wish to bring a pen and paper to jot down expressions of gratitude as you walk. I recommend the former for those who wish to establish a rhythm and pace fed by their gratitude, and I recommend the latter for those who seek a more reflective practice.

Whichever style of Gratitude Walk you choose to go on, you can express your gratitude in any of these ways: "I am thankful for …" "I have gratitude for …" "I am grateful for …" You choose what feels best for your walk.

Prior to beginning your Gratitude Walk, I encourage you to set an intention. For example, "With this walk, I will discover gratitude within and around me in ways that elevate my understanding of and appreciation for all life." Those aligned with prayer may wish to ask to be assisted in recognizing and embracing gratitude, and the places within them that have not yet been open to gratitude.

Once you have decided which version of the walk you will perform on this day, and you've set your intention, turn off your cellphone, switch it to airplane mode, or leave it behind.

Perform your GBS Pre-Walk Check-In.

Before you begin to walk, find gratitude in your *ability to walk*. Just hold that thought. This is a powerful starting point.

As you walk, remain connected to the ground; feel your steps as you keep your spine long and your head high, walking with your body, mind, and heart open and thankful, as you allow yourself to embody gratitude to whatever degree you can, realizing that it may feel strange, foreign, and even scary to you in the beginning.

If you are having trouble getting your gratitude flowing, you can begin your steps by saying aloud or to yourself whatever you are thankful for about your physical body: "I am thankful for my eyes that allow me to see," "I am thankful for my ears that allow me to hear," "I am thankful for my feet," etc. Or you may begin with something you see: "I am thankful for my car," "I am thankful for my home," "I am thankful for the sun," etc.

The entire time you walk, you will be coming up with things that you are thankful for.

You are going to saturate every cell in your body with gratitude.

If you are going on the faster gratitude walk, I encourage you to align your statements of gratitude with the rhythm of your steps; that is, with every step you take, issue a part of your statement of thanks: "I … am … thankful … for … the trees … and … the earth …."

If the moment occurs when your internal gratitude well begins to run dry, turn your focus outside and see what you can be thankful for or appreciate right in front of you—the path or walkway you're on, the clouds in the sky, the birds in the trees, etc.

Over the course of your walk, you may find yourself repeating things you have gratitude for. This is fine. It can only deepen the experience.

Also, find gratitude for things you never thought you would feel grateful for, like past challenges. For example: the boss who fired you, who actually did you a favor because you disliked the job and found a better-suited one; or the breakup or relationship that was tough, but taught you so much.

When something negative enters your thought-stream, perhaps even doubt about expressing gratitude, say, "I am thankful for my ability to spot negative thoughts. With gratitude for what it has taught me, I now release this thought." And give it a strong exhale as well.

Be creative with your thankfulness. Reach deeply into yourself—and allow yourself to be surprised.

As you conclude your walk, recognize any lightness that has entered you, along with any mental, physical, or emotional shifts. Allow gratitude to live in you for the rest of the day and beyond.

HOW TO DO: FOR TWO OR MORE PEOPLE

In a culture where we are constantly tearing ourselves and others down, and often focusing on the negative, just knowing that you and others will be doing this walk makes me feel gratitude.

Assemble your group; it can be just you and one other person, or you and many.

Choose a location that fits well with your Gratitude Walk. You may wish to decide upon the particulars of the walk—the route, distance, etc.—prior to starting off; this way, the participants can more fully concentrate on their expressions of gratitude during the walk.

I've found that the Gratitude Walk for two or more people works very well when you partner up, one-to-one.

It can also be done as a group sharing experience, with gratitude expressed by participants about things that are close to them or the group itself.

There are two key elements to this walk: *expressing* and *listening*.

One person in the pairing (or group) expresses their gratitude while the other person (or group members) listens, then the switch takes place and the listener then shares and is listened to and received.

There are times when someone may just want to listen, or be a "designated listener," and has nothing to share on a particular day. Listening is very powerful, as is hearing and receiving what others have gratitude for. So this is perfectly fine. One day you may be someone's ideal designated listener.

Turn off your cellphone, switch it to airplane mode, or leave it behind.

Perform your GBS Pre-Walk Check-In.

Having established your pairings, and knowing who in the pairing will share first, begin your walk.

As you and your partner, or you and your group, proceed, you will listen, and hear, but not comment—unless commenting has been agreed upon—about what is being shared with you.

You will receive. You will reflect. You will see how and what another person's gratitude stirs within you.

Remember, this entire walk is positive. If you run out of things to express gratitude for, return to the foundation: "I am thankful for my voice to express myself," "I am thankful to have a friend walking beside me," "I am thankful for the air I breathe," etc.

Also, allow for silences, even long silences, as gratitude is felt and further discovered.

Conclude your Gratitude Walk knowing that you have expressed (and received) words, sentiments, and understandings that helped grow happiness, shift perspectives, and elevate the life experience of yourself and those in your presence.

TAKEAWAYS AND REFLECTIONS

What did you learn from your Gratitude Walk? Did your mood shift?

How did your body feel as you got deeper into your Gratitude Walk? Perhaps your breathing became fuller and easier? Were you already a thankful person? Did you come up with things (and "I am thankful for" steps) that surprised you or that you never expected?

Can you see how this practice will serve you well in the future?

If you did this walk with others, how did it feel to share gratitude with another?

Could you feel a shift within yourself as you shared your gratitude? Did you feel a shift—or an uplift—within the group?

What was it like to hear another person expressing their gratitude? Did it elevate your own walk, perhaps causing you to reflect?

Jot down or make mental notes of what may have arisen for you around gratitude, and return to the Gratitude Walk often. You can even do it every day in short segments throughout your day to help you make the shift into living in a greater state of thankfulness and gratitude.

Keeping a gratitude journal can be helpful as well.

WALK 24
Seeing Walk

The voyage of discovery is not in seeking new landscapes but in having new eyes.

—MARCEL PROUST

OVERVIEW

Take a walk outside your living space. What do you see?

Earlier in this book, you were introduced to Walking Awake through Your Living Space (page 65). The purpose of that walk was to help you to become more aware of and awake to what has perhaps not been seen, felt, or noticed in a long time, if ever, within your living space, and to get you more in tune with your home environment.

The purpose of the Seeing Walk is for you to walk awake—fully engaged and *seeing*—through the outer world, starting directly outside your home, as well as in other areas you spend a great deal of time in and around (that have become routine and habitual), and then expand out to additional areas, be they parks, neighborhoods, school campuses, museums, or anyplace else you may wish to really "see."

Just as the Listening Walk (page 89) allowed you to tune into and hear sounds you had not heard before, and the Outer Smile Walk (page 85) encouraged you to connect with and show your appreciation to your external environment, you will now discover, and learn more about, your immediate outer world, or other locations, via your eyes.

This walk can be especially rewarding for pairs or groups, as everyone sees the world differently; and looking at the world through the eyes of another undoubtedly opens us to seeing objects, places, people, moments, and angles in a way we may not have seen on our own.

Embarking on this walk with others takes us into our everyday environment—and new environments—in a way that fosters greater discovery, understanding, and joy, from our combined vision.

It's a wonderful exercise for families, siblings, teams, work groups, couples, walking groups, and just about any other pairing one could come up with.

As I so deeply feel, and often express, those of us who can walk are blessed, as are those of us who can see. Let's not squander these blessings, but rather allow them to grow us.

BENEFITS

- Allows you to see what has gone unnoticed.
- Brings you into the present, and trains you to become aware.
- Grows your appreciation—or tells you what you'd like to change—about your immediate environment.
- Opens you to the wonders of the world.
- Strengthens one of the core ways you receive information.
- Helps you to better understand the world, and the life you've created, via what you now see.
- Slows you down.
- Can spark creativity.
- When performing with others, this walk can reveal more of the world through the eyes of others.
- Can help unite us in a common vision.
- Grows and teaches you, as an individual or as a group.

WHEN TO DO

- When needing to, desiring to, or ready to grow your connection to an environment you dwell within but never really notice or "see."
- When wanting to become more awake to and aware of your surroundings.
- When you recently moved into, or are visiting, a new environment.
- When needing to slow down, regroup, and just be with what is.

- When wanting to open yourself up to the wonders of the world.

- When a child (or adult) is bored, in need of focusing, or looking to explore.

- Perform this walk as a group whenever you wish to see more of the world through the eyes of others, or when you wish to learn more about how your friends or family see and become aware of their environments.

- Perform this walk as a team-building exercise.

HOW TO DO: ALONE

Begin with a strong intention to slow down and *see* the world now, acknowledging what is before you in a way that is like that of a visitor new to this planet, or someone who has just been given eyes to see.

You may wish to carry a notebook and a pen to jot down notes about what you see. If you are not recording notes, I recommend noting to yourself, whether silently or aloud, what you are observing.

You may even wish to set an intention of something you'd like to see or become aware of: "I will now see all that is for my highest good and deepening awareness to see." Those aligned with prayer may ask that they be shown all they need to see.

Pick your starting place. I suggest you first focus on your everyday walk: the routine walk to your car, train, or other means of transportation, or to your mailbox, campus, a friend's home, or the local market. Whatever your daily routine outside your home consists of, start with it, or a portion of it.

Turn off your cellphone, switch it to airplane mode, or leave it behind.

Perform your GBS Pre-Walk Check-In.

With your feet connected to the ground, and your awareness of the space around you established, begin to walk, slowly taking in the world through your eyes. (At times you may wish to engage soft eyes; see the Soft Gaze Walk, page 191, to add dimension to your Seeing Walk.)

Look at the first thing that meets your eyes—be it the steps, the sidewalk, or grass—and really see it. Acknowledge what you are seeing, either out loud or silently.

One by one, look at all the objects around you. Challenge yourself to look at everything, near and far, that may have previously gone unnoticed.

See the various colors and name them. See the shapes and forms and shadows and shafts of light. See what is new, and what is old and decaying.

Notice the lived moments occurring all around you and name them: "I see life." "I see movement."

Remain connected to your body and your breath as you continue to allow yourself to move slower than you usually do.

Notice what it feels like to really see your environment.

As you conclude your Seeing Walk, remember the words of Marcel Proust: "The voyage of discovery is not in seeking new landscapes but in having new eyes."

HOW TO DO: FOR TWO OR MORE PEOPLE

Assemble your seeing group, be it you and one other person, or many. Decide where you would like to embark on your Seeing Walk. Familiar grounds are always a good starting place, as they deepen your experience of them. The natural world in all its many forms can be a feast for the combined eye, as can a city.

You may wish to designate someone to carry a "seeing list" to catalogue all that is noticed. As mentioned in the Listening Walk (page 89), children really like the idea of a list; it gives them something to do, something to later reflect back on—and also provides a bit of structure. You may also choose to do this walk in silence, then later recall for one another what was seen.

Consider setting a group intention of something you'd like to see or become aware of. (For instance, a bird that is known to be in the area, or another sight or sights that intrigue and interest the group.)

Turn off your cellphone, switch it to airplane mode, or leave it behind.

Perform your GBS Pre-Walk Check-In.

Then begin to walk.

Remember, these walks are not to a set or prescribed distance; your group may end up walking many miles—if so desired—or a few hundred feet, or perhaps only twenty feet (there is often a great deal to see and discover in a twenty-foot space, when we are fully present).

As you walk, look around. Don't "strain" to see. But be "present" to see.

Let the pace and the walk be enjoyable and suit your family or walking group.

Tune into which sights are made by people, and which sights originate in the natural world.

I encourage you to shift between hard (or regular) focus and soft focus. (See the Soft Gaze Walk on page 191.)

Become aware of what you can see and identify versus what others in the group are seeing and identifying. As mentioned earlier, this walk can be done in silence, and at the end what has been seen is then discussed; or it can be done in silence with only gestures as a way of communicating what is seen; or you can choose to use your voices.

When you choose to speak throughout, you may wish to assign a location or direction for each sighting: "Classic car to our left," "Discarded bicycle wheel to the right," etc.

When the walk is done in silence, I suggest that each member of the group silently note to themselves what they are seeing.

If your group comes upon a sight that they love or that intrigues them, stay with it. Remember, it's more than fine to pause your walk to tune in and see deeper, and perhaps share some words.

Realize that depending on where you are, you may go for long stretches without seeing anything "new." When this is the case, continue to notice and be present to the familiar, but perhaps engage in a conversation that leads to a new way of seeing it.

You can also ask yourself and your fellow seers, "What don't you see?" And think of the sights that are absent, or absent from your everyday life.

When doing a there and back walk—not a loop but heading one way and then returning back the same way—I find it great to have kids see (and list what they see) on the way out, and then concentrate on (and list) what they do not see on the way back. An example would be if they're in nature, they won't see a TV, a video game, a billboard, a skateboard, or other items whose sights may have become woven into their everyday life. So ask them "What don't you see that you normally see?" on the return journey, and encourage them to write or verbally share a list.

Conclude your walk with a richer understanding of and deeper connection to your immediate surroundings or wherever you may have found yourself walking during your two-or-more-people Seeing Walk.

TAKEAWAYS AND REFLECTIONS

What was your Seeing Walk experience like? Did it visually reveal a lot to you about your everyday routine?

Were you able to notice or spot many things, be they made by people or of the natural world, that you had not seen before? Was it hard for you to slow down and focus on one thing at a time? Did you try the soft gaze approach as well, perhaps noticing things with your peripheral vision?

Do you feel you now have a better connection to the world you normally pass by?

What did you learn, not only about your environment but also about yourself?

If you practiced your Seeing Walk in a location that you have not been to before, do you feel it deeply enriched your time spent there?

If you performed the Seeing Walk as a group, were you surprised by anything that was discovered or pointed out by others? Did you find that you liked to be the one to spot something, or did you prefer to have others do the spotting?

If you walked as a group, did you perform the walk in silence, or did you speak? Was a seeing list created? Are there now other places, be they near or far, that you would like to *see* as a group?

Remember, seeing not only deepens your life experience, it is also a great tool for bringing you into the here-and-now present moment—no matter where you may find yourself.

Thank you for seeing life. As long as our eyes allow us to see, let us use them well.

WALK 25 Centering Walk
(a.k.a. Walking from Your Center)

My strength comes from my abdomen. It's the center of gravity and the source of real power.

—BRUCE LEE

OVERVIEW

"I'm feeling uncentered." "He's off his center." "She's totally centered."

The idea of being "centered" or "uncentered" in our daily lives is not uncommon. The first way we will address it here in the Centering Walk is the way in which it is most commonly known or referred to, and that has to do with a state of mind: You're feeling stressed; therefore, you are not feeling centered. You're feeling scared or nervous; therefore, you are not feeling centered. You're "feeling off"; therefore, you're not feeling centered.

To alleviate this situation, you (hopefully) learn to do things like slowing yourself down, working with your breath, planting your feet on the ground, meditating, maybe even taking a walk. This helps you to clear your mind, settle your nervous system, regain a sense of balance, and "get centered." All this will be a part of the Centering Walk. But there's also another form of being centered, one that is related to everything mentioned above, but is also more specific. It has to do with literally connecting with and moving from your actual center, or center of gravity.

The center of gravity is the place in a system or body where the weight is evenly dispersed and all sides are in balance.

Do you know where your center is? Or more specifically, can you locate your center of gravity?

The majority of us don't, and can't. If you fall into this category, the answer is: When you're standing, your center of gravity is located two inches—or three finger-widths—below your navel in the "center" of your abdomen.

Though it's mentioned in many sports, the center, or center of gravity, is most often discussed, and its virtues imparted, in the martial arts, specifically in aikido, tai chi, and qigong. It's often referred to as the *hara* in Japan and the *dantian* in China.

> *In Eastern philosophy, the hara or dantian is viewed as having physical, psychological, and spiritual elements. It is known as the "sea of qi," the true place of concentrated power or force within the body. We will touch on this a bit—and if you're so inclined, I encourage you to investigate further—but our main focus will be on how to connect more readily into our center of gravity, and move from this place.*

First, what takes you out of your center?

For the most part, it's worry, fear, stress, overthinking—some would even say modern life itself. And where do these things reside? The majority, although affecting the entirety of you, is guided by your thoughts, your head. When you depart the head and drop down deeper into the body, be it the heart, or the center point, not only do you establish more balance, but you also invite in fresh and needed perspective, while often quieting your thoughts.

This rings true for me. I find that when things are off or "out of whack" with my body, it's usually because my head is controlling everything—my head has become my center—and I've lost out on the balance, ease, and wisdom of the body.

Interestingly, what has been called the second brain, or the enteric brain, which is part of the gut and often responsible for that "gut feeling," is more readily available to us when we are centered.

The Japanese have an expression, *koshi ga takai mono,* which translates to "a person with high hips," meaning that that person is not in a place of centered balance and strength.

Being "in your head" or "having high hips" weakens you. But when you cultivate "dropped attention"—when your attention is directed toward your center, along with the powerful area of the hips and pelvis, and all the way down to the earth—you become not only more stable, but also more fluid. (There's a big difference between leaning into a situation with your head, and stepping or moving into a situation from your center. Try it.) Discussions and demonstrations of the center often present the "test your center of gravity techniques." One of the more common is to stand in front of a person with your attention focused in your head, and have the person give you a light push or shove, then do the same with your attention focused on your center. The result is always the same: you feel more stable, and are less easily moved, when you are focused on your center.

It's not so much that you have to continually live in your center, but that you develop the ability to continually *return to your center*, whatever the circumstance or situation.

The Centering Walk will help you to develop dropped attention and establish a conscious connection to your center.

This walk benefits children as well, and is a terrific way to introduce them to the concept of "being centered."

BENEFITS

- Helps you to relax and release tension.
- Helps you to better maintain a state of balance.
- Brings you more stability and a feeling of rootedness, yet also buoyancy.
- Tends to open your breathing.
- Being centered brings with it a deeper connection to inner clarity, wisdom, and equipoise.
- Allows you to move and sense in a more intuitive manner.
- Helps you to improve posture and feel less "wobbly."
- Connects you to a place of power.

WHEN TO DO

- When needing to feel centered.

- When wanting to improve upon your connection to your center of gravity and a place of more ease.

- When wanting to steer your focus out of your head and into your center.

- When wanting to explore movement in a more fluid manner.

- When wanting to feel stronger and more stable in your stance or walk.

- When wanting to improve your posture.

- When wanting to deepen your breathing.

- When curious about the energetic system, or qi, within your body.

- When wanting to empty out anything that keeps you from being centered, or that keeps you from being in your original nature.

- When wanting to relax.

HOW TO DO

It can be beneficial to have a partner when engaging in the Centering Walk. A partner can provide cues to help keep you in your center, and also provide feedback regarding their observations of you and your walk. You can take turns cueing and observing one another.

Whether it be indoors or outdoors, select a starting point for your walk.

Select shoes without a pronounced heel. You may also wish to walk barefoot when the location is appropriate.

A valuable affirmation to include with your Centering Walk may be: "Stable, fluid, and balanced, I move from my center with ease."

Turn off your cellphone, switch it to airplane mode, or leave it behind.

Perform your GBS Pre-Walk Check-In. Be sure to have your feet shoulder-width apart.

Now set your mind—or apply "dropped attention"—on your center.

One of the ways to assist in doing this is to *place your index finger on the area two inches—or three finger-widths—below your navel.* (To further assist in locating your center, place the index finger of your opposite hand on the spot on your back directly in line with your finger in the front. Envision them meeting at the center of the abdomen, halfway between the two fingers.)

With your finger(s) in place, continue to tune into your center and see if you can relax even deeper, and perhaps even easier—softening your eyes, and relaxing your jaw, neck, shoulders, abdominals, thighs, and anywhere else you may be holding tension.

Lean forward, then lean back. Remain focused on your center as you do. Then come to rest in the middle.

Now close your eyes and continue standing in the middle, tuning into your center, becoming *still* in your center. With your spine long, with equal weight on each foot, and with your center visualized, move your hips a few times from front to back and side to side. See how connecting with your center affects your stance and your posture, and see what it is like to allow your body to organize around this space, and then ultimately walk from this place.

As you ready yourself to walk, it must be noted that there is no *physical body part* that represents your center, so it's up to you to come up with something to envision. Some effective visuals that I've heard over the years are: a "glowing ball," an "arrow," a "shining pearl," a "small steering wheel." You can pick one of these, or a visual image of your own, and envision it to be your center point.

Pick a location somewhere in front of you. For example, if indoors, pick a point at the other side of the room; if outdoors, pick a tree or other object. You are going to walk toward it, but you will do so from (and with) your center.

Focus your center point on the destination, and have your center point lead you there.

For most of us, this requires a new type of focus. And it may feel odd, since you may have never walked with your mental focus anywhere else but in your head, focusing solely from behind your eyes. But soon, if it does not happen immediately, you will see that it becomes quite natural—and may even immediately feel good.

As you walk, remain aware of your footsteps, your breath moving in and out of your belly, and the workings of your legs, hips, and pelvis as you continue to select places to walk toward—or just walk in general—allowing the glowing ball, or whatever you've chosen, to lead.

When you turn around, you can envision your center point turning.

Walk whatever distance and length of time you prefer. Remember, it's not about having to always remain in your center, but about being able to return to it when you lose it. (To assist you, use the breath, your chosen visual image, and the touch of your finger(s) two inches below the navel.)

Take turns alternating between your regular walk (with focus coming from behind your eyes) and your dropped attention, Centering Walk. Pay attention to what you notice.

Observe your thoughts, feelings, and emotions while walking from your center.

Keep your spine long, feeling the linked connection between your head and pelvis, and keep your feet connected to the ground.

Allow your arms to move naturally as you walk.

No matter the distance chosen, or how successful this attempt was, complete your Centering Walk knowing that you have discovered a new way to move your body through space—and that's exciting.

Additional Practices You May Wish to Implement

Apply soft, relaxed eyes (see the Soft Gaze Walk on page 191) and then go back to your regular way of seeing.

Try this walk with your eyes closed. With your partner or a spotter at your side, close your eyes and walk from your center.

Allow your abdominals and core to remain soft as you allow your breath to wash through and connect into this place within you—your hara, dantian, or sea of qi—and see if you can allow this center space to radiate energy all the way out to your fingertips and toes, as you advance from your center.

Try walking up and down stairs from your center.

Try walking backward from your center.

As you become more comfortable with this type of walk, try tuning into and moving from your center when you're wearing a backpack, pushing a stroller, carrying groceries, etc.

TAKEAWAYS AND REFLECTIONS

What was your Centering Walk experience like? Were you able to connect to this specific space within you? If so, did it shift the way in which you stood? Did you feel more stable, more connected to your legs? How did your body feel when you walked from your center point?

Could you feel yourself—and perhaps your thoughts—leaving your head and becoming more embodied and centered? Did you perhaps feel a bit taller? Lighter? Less stressed? More grounded? Did it improve your posture, or give you greater awareness of your posture?

Did you sense or feel a connection to the concentrated place of power—or sea of qi—in your center?

Remember, your connection to your center is most available to you when you are present and relaxed. And you are most present and relaxed when you are aware of—and dropped down into—your center. As stated earlier, breath awareness is a helpful tool for keeping you in your center—as is visualizing your center point and occasionally touching the area two inches below your navel throughout your day.

Jot down or make mental notes of any takeaways and reflections you may have relating to your Centering Walk. Like all things new to you, being centered—and moving from or with your center—takes practice. But in this case, the practice itself is of great value. As always, there is no perfection, and your center knows this, so don't make it hard on yourself.

Whether it be in the physical, psychological, or spiritual sense, your center is always there for you.

WALK 26
Crowd Walking

If you want to conquer the anxiety of life, live in the moment, live in the breath.

—AMIT RAY

OVERVIEW

Do you like to walk in crowds or among masses of people? No one does, right? Actually, I've found that there are many people who not only enjoy walking in and through crowds of people, and in bustling cities in general, but find it energizing.

You may never become one of those people, but you can certainly develop the tools and a greater mind-body understanding that will enable you to at least flow better when you find yourself in a Crowd Walking situation, which for many of you might be quite often.

I spoke earlier about how my elementary school teachers would often have us line up single-file when walking to class, and how they would also try to control the group, for obvious reasons, when the pace got a little too quick or the energy and excitement grew beyond their liking. However, as we know, there are no teachers calling out commands when we are walking along a crowded city street, or other crowded area. It's pretty much a free-for-all.

I also mentioned earlier how I enjoyed walking in New York City, and how before I would engage with the masses, I would take time to ground and center myself and connect with my breath and the space around me. You learned that very technique, GBS, in chapter 5, "Before You Walk." This is immensely helpful when dealing with free-for-all, "uncontrollable" situations.

You may always seek out or select the less-traveled road, path, lane, or sidewalk. That's fine. But you may also find yourself in moments when that's not an option. Or you may find, and even regret, that you've limited the places you've visited in the past due to their crowded nature.

Sometimes taking the path less traveled has benefits, and sometimes taking the path most traveled has benefits. I've found we grow best, or best put into practice what we've learned, when challenged by others and/or our environment. I'm excited to share this walk, knowing that we can turn walking in crowds into an awareness-building meditation that will serve us well.

As for *my* most challenging Crowd Walking (and standing) experience, it would have to have been when I was a senior in high school and went into New York City on New Year's Eve to watch the ball drop in Times Square. If I recall correctly, that was anything *but* a meditation.

BENEFITS

- Better prepares you for walking with and interacting with crowds of people.

- Informs you how (and who) you are in Crowd Walking situations.

- Reveals to you and allows you to strengthen how you connect into, and own—or do not own—your personal space.

- Helps you thrive in your own space.

- Gives you tools and understanding to better navigate, both physically and mentally, movement happening around you, and within you.

WHEN TO DO

- When you find yourself walking in a crowded location, or know you will soon be doing so.

- When you want to grow your comfort zone in the midst of crowds.

- When wanting to further hone your awareness of how you move, act, and react when among the masses.

- When you want to observe how others move, interact, and live in their body and personal space while engaged in a crowd or group of moving bodies.

- When you are ready to claim more of your personal space and identity in the world.

HOW TO DO

I realize that some of you reading this may be highly empathic or sensitive in nature, and being among crowds or groups of people can be challenging, and at times nearly impossible. Others of you may have an anxiety-inducing fear of crowds. As with everything in this book, go at your own pace, ensuring your personal well-being. But also remember that stress in small doses actually makes us more robust.

Begin by asking yourself the following questions, with the intention of determining who you are currently when walking in a crowd. Some of these may best be answered in real-time Crowd Walking situations.

- What is your relation to walking in crowds or being in crowds in general? Is it something you've never been comfortable with? Is it something you've always loved? Is it something you've learned to tolerate? Or is it something that "just is" and you have never given it any thought?

- Where do your eyes go? Do you tend to make eye contact?

- Do you feel centered and grounded when in the midst of a crowd? Or do you feel uncentered, unmoored, and at the mercy of the crowd?

- Physically, do you puff yourself up, making yourself bigger? Or do you perhaps shrink yourself down, making yourself less noticeable?

- How do you feel when you are in a crowd: Calm? Anxious? Angry? Scared? Do you get excited?

- Do you hold yourself back, deferring space to others, even beyond politeness? Or do you perhaps invade others' space—often without even knowing so until you bump them or get too close?

- Do you get super focused on your own path and positioning, mapping out your next steps? Or do you just follow the movement of the crowd?

- How do you find yourself breathing when walking within or through a crowd? Do you hold your breath, and just go for it? Do you consciously breathe throughout? Or do you have no idea how you breathe when in a crowd?

After you have given some thought to these questions and grown your awareness of who you are in a crowd, it is time to focus on some tools and steps to assist you with Crowd Walking.

First, realize that as humans we tend to look for the path of least resistance. That's natural and is hardwired into most of us. So the question is: Can we find the path of least resistance, *even within a crowd?* I say yes. And that's our goal.

There are many factors that contribute to how you deal with crowded situations. Though each walk and crowd is unique, the suggestions presented below can be thought of as a one-size-fits-all method for becoming more capable and present while walking in a crowd.

More so than with any of the other walks in this book, awareness is key: awareness of self, of others, and of the environment. With this in mind, your GBS Pre-Walk Check-In (which can be done on the fly and much quicker when need be) is a crucial tool. The second most important thing is flow—finding your place within it.

Tools and Steps to Assist You with Crowd Walking

Perform your GBS Pre-Walk Check-In.

Remain loose and fluid. When entering a crowd, the norm is to unconsciously constrict, tighten, and make ourselves small, even invisible. Those who enjoy, or are not adversely affected while, walking in crowds do the opposite of this. While remaining conscious of the space of others, they remain full in their energy. *And* they remain fluid—less rock, more water. (Don't worry, "less rock" does not mean more vulnerable; remember, when you are fluid, you are far more present and able to respond to multidirectional challenges in a dynamic manner.)

Some practical ways to do this are to soften your jaw, relax your shoulders, allow your spine to be long and your neck to be free, and breathe.

You can also use an affirmation; for example, "I hold my ground and claim my space no matter the energies around me." Or a simpler affirmation: "I am safe." Or "I flow with strength and ease."

Whenever possible, choose your entry point and your exit point—it may be the one thing you can "control." Even though the goal is to remain "in the moment," it's always good to set a visual course to the point you want to reach; this could be in small sections, say city block by city block, or focusing on a landmark far in the distance. When *you* know where you're going, it helps others to know where you're going.

Once you know your destination, you may wish to take a few moments to visualize yourself finding the path of least resistance, and moving with little to no effort through the crowd.

Remain aware of and connected to your center—the area *two inches below your navel in the center of your abdomen* (see the Centering Walk, page 165)—and try to operate from that point, leading your movements from your center.

Continue to remain aware of the ground beneath you, the breath within you, and the space around you—including your full energy body. And at times, *ride your breath through the spaces in the crowd.*

Additional Tools You May Wish to Implement during Your Crowd Walking

Count off "left" and "right" steps. Some people find it helpful to count off steps in their head: left foot … right foot … left foot … right foot … being aware of each footfall.

Incorporate a soft gaze. You may wish to incorporate a soft gaze. (See the Soft Gaze Walk, page 191.) Softening your gaze can greatly enhance your peripheral vision and your sensing, and also help you to remain relaxed.

Practice movement. Unlike regular walking, which is predominantly forward with some weaving here and there, walking in a crowd can take you in many directions—side to side, backward, stop, forward again—all within seconds. So it's helpful to be comfortable moving in different directions nearly instantaneously. This can be practiced, and in a fun way. Many of the other walks in this book—including the Slow Motion Walk (page 186) and the Turning and Tilting Your Head Balance Walk (page 61)—can be very helpful.

I encourage you to continue to look for ways to bring more ease, flow, and awareness into your crowd walking experiences—and all your experiences—holding your space, and your center, while mixing with the masses.

TAKEAWAYS AND REFLECTIONS

What did reading about and working with Crowd Walking teach you about yourself? Were you able to answer the questions posed to you? If so, were you able to do so from memory and recollection, or did you engage them when in or near a crowd?

Did you search out a place to execute your Crowd Walking, or did you incorporate the techniques during your regular "crowded" walk?

If walking in a crowd has been challenging for you in the past, did you find it easier to do now? Were you able to grow your connection with your personal space and energy? Did you feel more "in control" while being less in control?

Did you become aware of the literal energy of the crowd, or the flow of the stream? Can you see how walking in a crowd can become a valuable form of meditation?

Jot down or make mental notes of any takeaways and reflections you may have. And know that whatever your experience, there will always be crowds out there to grow you.

WALK 27
Slow-Fast Walk

Sometimes you need to slow down to go fast.

—JEFF OLSON

OVERVIEW

Throughout this book, we have explored expanding awareness and increasing overall wellness through a myriad of walks. The Slow-Fast Walk is yet another way in which we will do so. Even though there is great room for awareness growing, and multiple wellness benefits to be had and discovered, the Slow-Fast Walk may also be considered the most "conventional" *exercise-focused* walk featured.

I actually consider this a mindfulness walk disguised as a fitness walk, since alternating between periods of high and low intensity, via interval style training, is great for fitness, but it's also great for developing mindfulness, *and* providing a mood-enhancing "mental lift" via the release of endorphins.

Do you prefer to walk fast or slow? Or do you like to mix it up?

When it comes to walking, especially exercise-related walks, we all have our preferred walking speed. Some of us push hard for the sake of our fitness goals or as a way to de-stress, and some of us go easier, so as to stave off injury or relax ourselves. Whether you push yourself hard or take it easier (or, in the case of this walk, mix the two), there is little debate that walking is among the safest and most effective forms of mind-body exercise.

Brain neuroplasticity (also known as brain plasticity) has revealed to us that the brain is capable of change throughout life, *and* we know that the body is very smart and adaptable. Therefore, the more we can do to vary our approach to fitness, and in this case, fitness through walking, the better.

There are times in life when we need to walk fast—whether it be in a burst or sustained—and it's good to know how we can best come into and go out of these moments in a way that works well for us, including *not losing ourselves* when we are moving fast.

Remember, it is the all of you, the entirety of you, that walks. And you'll want to continue to learn about, and grow, the *all of you*. Varying your speed while walking is a great way to do so.

In this "Fitbit" age when we can track our distance, time, steps, heart rate, etc., the Slow-Fast Walk can be highly effective and fun. But you certainly do not need a Fitbit or other device to receive the full mind-body benefits of the Slow-Fast Walk.

The following is the general structure of the Slow-Fast Walk, which can be adjusted to suit you better. For example, you can spend more time walking slow and less time walking fast, if that feels right for you, or more time walking fast and less time walking slow. Just remember to stay present, and truly tune in during your periods of fast walking.

GENERAL STRUCTURE OF THE SLOW-FAST WALK:

5 minutes slow. 1 minute fast.

3 minutes slow. 1 minute fast.

2 minutes slow. 1½ minutes fast.

2 minutes slow. 1 minute fast.

5 minutes slow.

Again, this is a guideline. You can extend the times (and repetitions) in any manner that serves you.

BENEFITS

- Improves your overall fitness levels.
- Deepens your connection to your body and movement.
- Helps elevate your mood via enhanced breathing and the release of endorphins.
- Reveals habits and patterns.
- Increases circulation and improves heart health.
- Increases energy, stimulates your metabolism, and burns calories.
- Reduces stress.
- May help reduce blood sugar (especially in type 2 diabetes)
- Helps the body to detoxify.
- Adds variety to your regular walking or fitness routine.

WHEN TO DO

- When needing to physically exercise.
- When wanting to elevate your mood.
- When wanting to improve your fitness.
- When wanting to lose weight.
- When needing to "de-stress."
- When needing to get outside and breathe.
- When wanting to grow your connection to your body.
- When wanting to learn more about yourself and the world around you while walking at varying speeds.
- The average Slow-Fast Walk will take twenty to twenty-five minutes to complete. It can be adjusted to be longer.

HOW TO DO

If you are new to fast walking (or what some may call power walking) or are not well conditioned, you may need to begin by keeping your fast-walking intervals to well under a minute. As your fitness levels improve, you can increase the amount of fast walking, along with the length of time you engage in it. I suggested an interval schedule in the Overview, that we will work from below, but that is simply a guideline.

While it is often suggested, from a pure fitness perspective, that you plan your interval times well in advance of your walk, I find it wiser to rather let each day, and how you are feeling, dictate your interval times. (As stated earlier, this walk provides you with many opportunities to grow your awareness. Part of that is tuning into and listening to your body.)

As you learned through many of the other walks, mindfulness and awareness are most readily revealed and increased when slowing yourself down. But the high art, with high rewards, is to be able to remain mindful and aware while moving much faster than you normally do.

DURING THIS WALK, KEEP THE FOLLOWING THINGS IN MIND:

How does your body move and feel when walking slowly versus walking fast? How do you experience the transitional moments (ramping up or ramping down) between slow and fast?

What are your thoughts like when you walk slowly versus when you walk fast? Do your thoughts drop away when you increase your speed and exertion for sixty to ninety seconds or longer?

As you speed up, your focus tends to be more locked in—think tunnel vision—and set on getting there, or accomplishing.

So the task at hand is to stay present, but expansive. Can you keep your focus open and expansive—remaining aware of your environment and yourself within it—while walking fast?

Can you burst forth and still remain connected to the rise and fall of your feet on the ground, and the way your clothes sound and feel as they move across your body?

Can you double or triple your speed and still allow your eyes to remain soft? (See the Soft Gaze Walk, page 191.)

Can you be as connected to—and in control of—your breath while you're moving fast as while you're moving slowly?

The Slow-Fast Walk provides the opportunity to discover these answers, and develop these abilities, and more.

Select your walking location and starting point.

Wear comfortable, well-fitting shoes. Dress appropriately, using layers if called for.

Hydrate with water prior to walking, and also bring water with you if you expect to walk for any significant time or distance, or if the weather dictates the need.

Set timers on your cellphone, watch, or Fitbit. Or you can just go by how you feel. (Unless you plan to utilize your cellphone for the walk, turn it off, switch it to airplane mode, or leave it behind.)

You can think of your difficulty levels on a scale of 1 to 10 (10 being the most difficult), and consider walking at 3 to 4 to be slow or normal, and 7 to 8 (and if you're up to it, 9) to be your target for fast walking.

One of the ways that you'll know when you're approaching maximum effort is that it will be hard for you to talk.

Perform your GBS Pre-Walk Check-In.

Begin your walk.

As you walk, think in terms of mind-body—or even mind-body-spirit—rather than just body.

Feel your feet on the ground. Keep your spine long. Keep your shoulders, hands, and jaw relaxed. Feel the entirety of you, including your hips, pelvis, and center (see the Centering Walk, page 165). Remain present to and aware of your surroundings.

Walk for 5 minutes at your slow or normal pace. Then increase to fast for 1 minute.

As you do, allow your hips and pelvis to rotate naturally as you speed up.

Allow your arms to move freely at your sides. Feel your arms moving through the air.

Allow your stride to naturally lengthen as you pick up your pace.

Take full breaths—in through the nose and out through the mouth.

Feel the energy—*your* energy—*your* vitality.

Try to remain as *present* to your body and your surroundings as you did while walking slower; that means *listening* as well.

Transition to slow walking for 3 minutes.

Remain mindfully aware of the transition periods as you go from higher exertion to lower exertion and back again.

Allow your heart rate and breathing to settle during the slow (or moderate) portions of your walk. Once again, stay connected to your feet rising from the ground and returning to the ground, your body moving through space, the sound and feel of your clothes, your breath, and the world around you.

Transition to your next 1 minute fast interval.

As you increase speed, feel the center line of your body as your hips and pelvis move and your legs and arms move in opposition to one another.

Bend your elbows to 90 degrees, and pump your arms as you walk.

Try to remain loose, even with your arms pumping at your sides.

Feel your breath, your lungs, your heartbeat, and your belly rising and falling with each inhale and exhale.

Remain aware of the terrain, cracks or rises in the sidewalk, roots on the trail, etc.

See how fast you can go without adding tension to your jaw or other parts of your body.

Allow your mood to lift as you increase your exertion and as your body releases feel-good hormones.

Transition to 2 minutes slow.

Remain present and aware. If you wish to or need to check your heart rate via your device, or manually, do so. But also tune into your aliveness in the moment; *feel* your heart beating within you.

Communicate to yourself what you are aware of: "That's my heartbeat," "Those are my lungs working," "That is sweat forming," etc.

Then ramp up again to 1½ minutes fast, followed by 2 minutes slow, followed by 1 minute fast, and concluding with 5 minutes slow.

Whether in your fast or slow interval, or in the transitions in between, continue to release tension and invite in ease.

Remember to cycle down by ending your walk with four to five minutes of slow walking. Feel your aliveness, feel your energy, breathe, and open your arms wide to life. And if you'd like, extend your time and keep walking at your normal pace, or you can segue into one of the other thirty-four walks.

TAKEAWAYS AND REFLECTIONS

Did anything surprise you about the Slow-Fast Walk? Did you find yourself challenged in any new ways? Did you learn anything new about yourself?

Were you able to feel connected to your center—both while walking slow and walking fast?

Were you able to remain connected to your breathing—both while walking slow and walking fast?

How did your body move and feel when walking slowly versus walking fast? How did you experience the transitional moments (ramping up or ramping down) between slow and fast?

Were your thoughts different while you walked slowly versus when you walked fast? Did your thoughts drop away when you increased your speed and exertion for that sixty to ninety seconds or longer?

If you have done this type of interval walk before, were you able to do it in a more mindful, aware manner now?

Can you see how this walk can help you to stay connected to yourself and your surroundings no matter what speed you're walking?

Jot down or make mental notes of any takeaways and reflections you may have. And work with the Slow-Fast Walk in ways, and at times, that you know will serve you best.

WALK 28
Slow Motion Walk

For fast-acting relief, try slowing down.

—LILY TOMLIN

OVERVIEW

When was the last time you walked in slow motion? By "walked in slow motion," I mean not when you were in pain or fatigued, but when you consciously made the choice to walk in an exaggerated slow manner.

For most of us, the answer is when we were a child, or more recently when we may have played with a child. For others of us, we may have reached deep into adulthood without having ever once walked, or moved, in slow motion.

Whatever the case, and whatever age you may be, you will now consciously explore this way of moving in your body, through space, that will add depth and richness to your regular-speed walk as it opens you to seeing, feeling, and experiencing your movements in a sloweddown and ultra-present manner.

We've all seen slow motion scenes in movies, and we are familiar with the idea of studying something—the movement of an animal, instant replays in sports, the function of a body part, or other "how-to" videos—that has been presented to us in slow motion.

You will now become the star of your own slow motion movie, and you will get to study yourself—and hopefully enjoy yourself—as the lead actor in this walking role.

Doing so can be as fun as it can be illuminating. And for kids, "super slow motion" often sounds cooler and more challenging, something they like.

We must realize that in this fast-paced world, *slow movement*, be it based in tai chi, Feldenkrais, or other styles of mindful, awarenessbased movement, has proved valuable time and time again for our greater overall health and well-being.

BENEFITS

- Slows you down and brings you into the present.
- Tunes you deeper into your walk, your body, and movement in general.
- Reconnects you to the spirit of play.
- Promotes balance, proprioception, and greater stability.
- Helps you to relax.
- Stimulates brain function.
- Can help you move from the sympathetic nervous system (fight or flight) to the parasympathetic nervous system.
- Teaches you that no matter the speed of the world, *you* can always slow down.

WHEN TO DO

- When needing to slow down.
- When needing to focus on (and in) the moment.
- When feeling overwhelmed.
- When wanting to tune deeper into your body and your walk, and perhaps uncover patterns and habits that you were unaware of.
- When wanting to work with and increase balance and stability.
- When wanting to have fun and explore slow motion walking by yourself, with kids, or in a group.
- This is a great way to help kids settle down, turning slowing down into a game of super-slo-mo "How slow can you go?"— while incorporating and encouraging some focused breathing as well.

HOW TO DO

Your Slow Motion Walk can be done anywhere. But it may serve you well to pick a location that makes you feel comfortable and does not draw unnecessary attention to yourself. For this reason, you may find it best suited to perform this walk indoors in your living space.

That said, a calm, inspiring spot in nature, a park, etc., can be highly beneficial.

Pick your location.

Turn off your cellphone, switch it to airplane mode, or leave it behind.

When appropriate, you can do this walk barefoot, allowing you to further "feel" your walk.

How slow is a slow motion? *Very slow.* Move just fast enough so you are continually in motion, yet slow enough to remain aware of your every movement and micro-movement. For many of you, this may indeed translate to "super slow motion." As a rule, when in doubt, go slower, but also realize that "slower" often translates to more difficult.

NOTE Surprisingly, slow motion walking can be challenging, especially balance-wise, since you are supported on one leg for most of the time. Try to remain fluid and even sleek (consider yourself more of a slow-moving cheetah than an old robot in need of oil). Remember to smile.

Perform your GBS Pre-Walk Check-In.

Just before you take your first step, *stop yourself.*

You will now fully engage, thinking and feeling/presencing your way through the entire chain of motion that occurs while walking— first by noticing what happens as you *set out to walk.*

As you begin your slow journey forward, the first thing to notice is what do you naturally move first?

For some people, it's their hand and arm that moves first, whereas others begin walking by first lifting their foot. Which did you do?

Whether your arm or your leg initiates the movement forward, notice that your opposite arm or leg (and side of the body) will go, to varying degrees, backward, because we naturally move in a contralateral manner. So remain aware of both sides of your body as the movement forward begins.

Staying connected to your breathing, begin another step.

Slowly lift your foot off the ground, feeling the weight leave the ground, move the foot and leg slowly through space—feeling your way through your entire body—then lower it, feeling the weight of your front foot once again meeting the ground as your back foot now prepares to advance.

Begin to slowly peel the back foot from the ground, setting off a cascade of movement, bringing it forward.

Be fully present throughout, recognize pivotal moments (like when you are on the heel of your front foot and the ball of your back foot), notice where your hands, arms, and torso are at this point, notice your breathing, and notice where your head is throughout.

As you continue, look for any sensations, kinks in the movement, sweet spots (where it may feel effortless), and anything else you can tune into, including emotions, and what type of thoughts arise.

Take ten or so steps like this, or more if you'd like, then turn around and head back to your original starting position. Repeat any number of times.

When you complete your Slow Motion Walk, return in a fully present way to your regular walk and see how it feels.

Additional Practices You May Wish to Implement during Your Slow Motion Walk

If you are feeling more adventurous, and have a handrail or spotter nearby, try walking up and down stairs in slow motion.

You can also try closing your eyes throughout parts or all of one or two complete steps, and therefore fully rely on your feeling and sensing. (But again, unless you are proficient in your balance, I encourage you to have a spotter nearby.)

Once you've recognized and executed your normal walk in a slow motion manner, and perhaps tried some stair walking, I encourage you to free yourself up to play a bit more by breaking out of your set walking pattern. You'll do this by allowing your arms and legs to travel in a very free manner, moving them in any way that is fun for you, and also in ways that may challenge you. You can even add some sound effects to your Slow Motion Walk, creating your own slow motion soundtrack.

Another valuable slow motion practice is to pretend you're falling—either to the side, forward, or backward—while slow motion walking, and then see how you recover yourself from this faux, slow motion fall. Remain aware of your body and breath as you go through the off-balance falling motion and correction.

Earlier I spoke of starring in your own slow motion movie. I mentioned that as a frame of reference. But I will also add here that it can be highly beneficial to record yourself, or have someone else record you, as you perform your slow motion walk. You can then go back and review it and learn.

Feel free to run in slow motion as well.

TAKEAWAYS AND REFLECTIONS

What did you learn from your Slow Motion Walk? Were you able to really tune into your movements? Was it fun? Informative?

Did you find it to be challenging? How was your breathing throughout? If it was not challenging, were you able to find a way to make it so? Did you allow yourself to be silly? Could you make it elegant? Did you try the stairs in slow motion?

How did it feel to return to your regular walk? Were you more present and connected to your body?

Revisit the Slow Motion Walk whenever you need to for its many benefits, including whenever you need to slow down your internal and external world.

Remember, for the most part, you control the speed at which you move through life. Always realize that you have more than one speed.

WALK 29
Soft Gaze Walk

If you change the way you look at things, the things you look at change.

—WAYNE DYER

OVERVIEW

How you look at the world is how you see the world, and there's more than one way to look at the world.

The Soft Gaze Walk invites you to see and experience your surroundings in a new way. Rather than allowing your focus to fix (hard focus) fully on one thing, object, or person, which is the norm, soften (relax) your eyes to see that one thing, but not to the exclusion of everything else. In other words, your soft gaze/soft eyes take in much more.

It is the same "soft eyes" principle used in many martial arts, perhaps most commonly in aikido, which allows participants to see, sense, and engage with a larger field of vision, limiting surprise attacks, etc.

Softening your gaze opens you up to life, expands your breath, heightens your senses, and often "takes the edge off."

In a society that is now focused for hours on end on small electronic screens, the Soft Gaze Walk not only is highly beneficial, it's highly needed.

On a personal note, one of the exercises I begin each of my Writing Into The Now workshops with is a hard focus/soft gaze exercise, where I begin by having participants focus intently on an object in the distance, then have them slowly soften their gaze—while still looking at the object—to include more and more of the world around them. We do three or four cycles of this. Participants find that it relaxes them and opens them up to greater receptivity.

The Soft Gaze Walk can be done while wearing your prescription eyewear. Depending on the strength of your prescription and your level of reliance on your eyewear, you may want to experiment with removing your eyewear.

BENEFITS

- Relaxes your eyes.

- Allows you to see, experience, and engage in your surroundings in a much broader way.

- Expands your vision to include the previously unseen.

- Helps you to relax, breathe more fully, and open yourself up both physically and mentally.

- Gives you "fresh eyes" and a new perspective when engaged in a project or process.

- Takes the hard edge off the world.

- Helps children (and adults) to let go of current obsessions or fixations.

- Helps reset and rest your eyes when engaged in computer/ screen work.

- Reduces stress.

- Often improves balance, and movement in general.

WHEN TO DO

- When you have been overly focused (mentally and *visually*) on a task.

- When you need a larger, clearer, or newer perspective on something, or what you may call "fresh eyes."

- When feeling tense, constricted, and needing to relax and unwind.

- When working for extended periods on a computer. (If you can't break away for a walk, look away from the screen and take a two- to three-minute soft gaze break. You will find that your breathing will naturally deepen as your field of vision opens.)

- When you wish to see, experience, and engage with more of your immediate surroundings.

- When you seek to expand your breath and breathing and calm your nervous system.

- When desiring to be open and omnidirectional in each moment.

- The Soft Gaze Walk is highly effective for children who have become "obsessed" or overly focused on something, as it provides a way for them to open up (and often release) without even realizing they did so.

HOW TO DO

Pick a location. It could be your immediate neighborhood, it could be inside or outside your office building or school, or it could be in a park, forest, or other natural setting.

Turn off your cellphone, switch it to airplane mode, or leave it behind.

Perform your GBS Pre-Walk Check-In.

As you continue to sense the space around you, begin to soften (relax) your eyes. While doing this, you may feel your face and jaw, along with other parts of your body, begin to relax and soften, coinciding with the softening of your gaze.

Breathe, and allow this softening of your eyes to assist you in sensing the space around you.

Now while standing still, grounded, tall, and aware of the space around you, begin to look around. You will notice that things may not be as crisp, and may even appear a bit fuzzy (or soft), as you soften your gaze.

Focus on items and objects at various distances, but don't "hard focus" on them. See them, but not to the exclusion of what else is around them. For example, if your soft gaze lands on a tree, see and focus on the trunk, but also the branches extending from the trunk.

Once this feels comfortable to you, begin your walk. Walk as far or short a distance as you'd like. As you walk, look at familiar sights and objects in this softer, more relaxed manner.

Allow yourself to be receptive to seeing and receiving visual information in this broader, softer way. Also allow yourself to be open to inspiration, greater clarity, and ease of movement.

For many of you, walking with a soft gaze may feel strange at first, as if you're entering a different world. Just be with it. Don't push, overthink, or overanalyze. Remember, with all these walks, it's about "presence," not perfection.

Have fun with this process. Allow yourself to enjoy it. Let it restore you, and perhaps let you see beyond what is normally obvious to you.

During your walk and upon completion, know that you are doing something good for yourself; namely, increasing your awareness and lived experience by relaxing—and trying less hard. Once again, think *from rock to water.* Only now, the softening takes place in your eyes, and works its way through the entirety of you.

Just like your breath, may the soft gaze become a tool that serves you well.

TAKEAWAYS AND REFLECTIONS

What was your experience like while performing the Soft Gaze Walk? Did things, objects, or your environment seem or appear different to you? Did you appear different to you? Were you comfortable? Did it relax you? Did your eyes feel better? Can you see how this practice can serve you well throughout your day?

In general, do you find yourself being more of a hard gazer, hard eyes type of person, or do you lean more toward soft eyes?

From this day forth, know that you always have a choice of how you look at the world.

WALK 30
Backward Walk

When you reach the end of what you should know, you
will be at the beginning of what you should sense.

—KAHLIL GIBRAN, *Sand and Foam*

OVERVIEW

Why walk backward? Because it teaches you more about how you walk forward. *And* it allows you to grow greater awareness and your ability to sense where you are in space and how you move through space.

It challenges and strengthens your balance and coordination. It engages the body and individual muscles in new ways. It shifts and expands your focus, stimulates the brain, and creates new neural pathways.

This walk is about learning and discovering. You learn and discover best—and awaken from autopilot—when you go slowly. As with many of the other walks in this book, think *slow and present,* rather than "I have to be able to do this with the same ease and ability as my forward walking."

Just as it is beneficial to learn how to mindfully walk from a slow to a fast pace (see Slow-Fast Walk, page 178), it is also very beneficial for you to cultivate the ability to go from walking forward to backward to forward again in a manner in which you remain as aware, connected, and fluid as possible.

This walk can be a fun addition to your existing walking or exercise routine, and it's great to do as a family (kids enjoy it) or walking group.

From a fitness point of view, you burn more calories and stimulate your cardiovascular system to a greater degree walking backward than forward.

BENEFITS

- Heightens your senses in many ways, including increasing proprioception.

- Increases your balance and improves concentration. ·

- From head to toe, it engages the mind-body, and individual joints and muscles, in new ways.

- Provides a greater understanding of, and often a new level of ease to, your forward walk.

- Slows you down and brings you into the present.

- Creates new neural pathways.

- Adds variety to your existing walking routine.

- Opens you to thinking and seeing in new ways.

- Can greatly improve sports performance.

- Many people who experience knee pain while walking forward do not experience it while walking backward.

- From a fitness perspective, your heart rate is elevated quicker while walking backward than forward, so the Backward Walk can be an excellent walk for cardiovascular conditioning. Backward walking also burns more calories than forward walking.

WHEN TO DO

- When wanting to engage and stimulate your body and mind in a new way.

- When wanting to improve your sensing abilities, balance, and concentration.

- When wanting to experience walking in a nonhabitual way.

- When wanting to greater connect with and bring more ease into your regular forward walk.

- When wanting to view the world from a different perspective.

- When wanting to add variety—or a fun and productive challenge—to your regular walking routine.
- When wanting to increase your fitness levels.

HOW TO DO

Select an area indoors or outdoors where you can safely alternate between walking forward and backward, such as a clear room, walkway, beach, field, or parking lot. You may wish to perform this walk on an indoor or outdoor track, as it provides an even surface, a controlled environment, and marked lanes.

When you grow more comfortable and capable with your backward walking, you may wish to engage in this activity on different terrains and varied surfaces; but always put safety first. With this said, consider having a spotter at your side if you feel at all uncomfortable or unstable walking backward.

When walking with a partner or group, you can take turns walking backward. The person walking forward (or observing/spotting) can also alert the backward walker to any potential trip hazards.

There are two ways you can perform this walk.

The first, and easier, is a back and forth walk that begins while facing (and walking) backward, then without turning around, walk in your regular forward manner back to your starting point, pause, and begin again. This can be done five to six times, taking fifteen to twenty steps each time.

The second way is to begin by walking in your regular forward manner and then turn around while walking, and begin walking backward. You will then alternate between forward and backward walking for ten to fifteen steps each way. When performing the walk in this manner, alternate which way you turn around to go backward—left one time, then right, then left, then right, etc.—and forward again.

Whichever variation you choose, the following steps/distances are only suggestions. Walk in whichever way feels best to you, and to whatever distance feels best. Just remember that you can learn a great deal from going a short distance slowly.

As you walk, pay attention to not only how you walk backward, but how you transition from forward to backward, and all you notice and sense as you walk. Notice that when you walk backward, the toes meet the ground first, yet when you walk forward, the heel strikes the ground first. All aspects of the walk are of equal importance.

When possible, walk in bare feet; otherwise, wear well-fitting shoes, and make sure your laces are securely tied.

Perform your GBS Pre-Walk Check-In. Really sense into the space behind you, feeling with your imagination, your mind's eye, and any other sensing ability you feel connected to, *including feeling your personal energy filling the space behind you.*

Whether you choose to perform the Backward Walk as first described, in a back and forth style, or as part of a conventional walk, where you alternate between forward and backward walking, these are the principles to engage in:

Go slow. Especially at first. Your first pass at walking backward should be done "just as you are," meaning in your raw, noninstructed state, just to see how it feels, and what it can grow into when you allow for further awareness and discovery.

Feel. From the bottom of your feet to the top of your head, feel what is happening with your body as you walk backward, then forward, and throughout your transitions. (You can even touch the different parts of the body that you are feeling, identifying the muscles or other areas that you are aware of.)

Sense. Sense the space behind you, to each side of you, and in front of you.

Pause. Pause at various points during your Backward walk, allowing you to see where you are within the motion.

Remain aware of your hips, your pelvis, and the midline (or vertical center line) of your body as you walk.

Breathe. Keep the body (including your jaw) relaxed.

Be aware of your mental state. If and when you feel frustrated, remind yourself, "I am exploring something new."

Have fun. Allow for a sense of play.

Always seek to make your Backward Walk more elegant and refined.

Conclude your Backward Walk by walking forward in a tuned-in and present manner.

TAKEAWAYS AND REFLECTIONS

What was your Backward Walk experience like? Did it feel odd? Have you done backward walking before? If so, was it different this time, having placed greater emphasis on the mindfulness/awareness aspect of the walk?

Did you become more comfortable walking backward? Did you feel as if you were developing, or connecting deeper into, the sensing mechanisms of your mind-body?

Did you feel your muscles, hamstrings, thighs, and calves working differently when you switched from forward to backward?

How did it feel when you switched back to forward? Did you feel a bit more ease enter into your walk? Perhaps a stronger connection to your hips and pelvis, and the ground beneath you?

Did your walking space or environment appear different to you while walking backward? Did you notice, sense, or feel things—whether they be physical, mental, emotional, or spiritual—that you may not have noticed, sensed, or felt before?

Jot down or make mental notes of any takeaways and reflections you may have. And return to the Backward Walk often.

WALK 31
Grieving Walk

Your grief path is yours alone, and no one else can walk it, and no one else can understand it.

—TERRI IRWIN

OVERVIEW

Grieving can be confusing, unsettling, scary, stressful, and often exhausting. When someone or something that we love leaves us, there is often a hole left behind. When our familiar activities and experiences are radically altered, we sometimes feel it directly in our hearts, and other times we experience an emptiness in the world around us. We question many things, including the meaning of life, our own destinies, our coping skills, our ability to change, and what the future holds for us.

Walking, especially in a natural setting, is healing, soothing, centering, and proved to reduce stress. Walking is also a wonderful way to show you how to move forward, while also honoring all that was.

It simply is one of the best therapies you can engage in.

As the father of modern medicine, Hippocrates, said, "Walking is the best medicine."

When grieving, our world tends to get smaller and smaller, often leaving us focused on a few moments in time, over and over. It also tends to have a way of tightening our body, as we constrict due to fear, stress, sadness, loneliness, fatigue, or uncertainty about the future.

Movement in general, whether it be dance, yoga, jogging, swimming, etc., can help you release tension and muscular and mental contractions brought on by loss and fear, and can open you up in a way that feels safe to you. But the above activities require a focus and energy that may not be available to you while grieving.

A Grieving Walk takes you on a gentle journey of healing, rediscovery, celebration, letting go, opening, and breathing, all the while allowing you to honor in the highest way what has left you.

Change and impermanence are a part of the human experience. Whether we are grieving or not, we are all constantly learning how to better let go and to be with what is. May this walk serve you on your healing journey.

When ready, you may wish to engage in a Dedication Walk (see page 137) in dedication or tribute to the someone or something that has departed. Many people have gone on to walk tremendous distances in honor of, and in tribute and dedication to, another. The Camino de Santiago—the old pilgrim route that goes from the Pyrenees right across Spain ending at the city of Santiago de Compostela—is one such route that is often traveled by the bereaved or in dedication to another.

If seeking additional support, there are walking groups available for those who are grieving.

BENEFITS

- Helps you to heal.

- Gets you back out into the world.

- Settles your mind and helps you to see things more clearly.

- Allows you to take action toward your own well-being.

- Releases hormones that allow you to feel happier and more hope-filled.

- Moves and opens your body, helping you to release stagnant energy and unrealized emotion.

- When with another or a group, it brings you much-needed support and allows you to be heard.

- Teaches you that life is continually in motion, and every ending— and step—is a new beginning.

WHEN TO DO

- When you are grieving the loss of a person or something else close to you.

- When you feel—or know—it is time to get out and move your body.

- When you have a partner or walking group to offer support, even if it's silent support, in your grieving.

- When wanting to elevate your mood.

- When wanting to help your mind unwind, so you can regain mental clarity.

- When wanting to embrace hope by seeing that the world truly does go on.

- When wanting to reenergize yourself.

- Self-care, or self-nurturing, is a big part of our return to wellness while grieving. And it is often neglected. Do this walk as a way of nurturing yourself.

- And of course you can walk your loved one's favorite walk.

HOW TO DO

Connect with a friend, a walking group for the grieving, or a hospice service that offers walking groups for those who are grieving.

Or you may choose to walk on your own. This may be exactly what you need. But do know that support is always available, and sometimes it makes it easier to commit to a walk when we know someone is waiting for us.

As for location, if and when possible, select a place to walk that is calming for you: a quiet neighborhood, a park, a beach, a garden path, a stretch of green grass, anyplace that will allow you to feel comfortable.

You may choose to carry an item with you that has significance, or gives you strength, perhaps placing it in a pocket to allow you to feel inspired, supported, or connected to that special someone or something. (You may at some point choose to leave this special item someplace worthy of it, or just leave it behind as the need and desire to carry it diminishes.)

If you'd like to use an affirmation while walking, an example may be: "With each step I take, I find peace." Or simply: "I am safe."

For those aligned with prayer, you may wish to ask for assistance in this grieving and mourning process: to bring you the strength, peace, and insight needed to move forward. Or simply ask: "As I take these steps, reveal to me what other steps I need to take."

Start slow. Walking for five minutes may be more than enough at first. (For some of us, just walking twenty feet to the mailbox or car may be a challenge at first.)

Carry some water, tea, or juice with you, perhaps some tissues, or anything else—including your cellphone—that makes you feel less vulnerable and more comfortable.

Begin by acknowledging and thanking yourself for taking these walking steps to assist in your healing.

Once you have your starting point, if you feel up to it, perform your GBS Pre-Walk Check-In.

Breathe. Relax your shoulders. Open your chest/heart area. Be gentle with yourself.

As you walk, feel your feet on the ground. Feel the *support* of the ground.

Let your eyes focus on what they wish to focus on, but do allow them to look around, to see the world in motion. See the vastness of the sky, and the cycles of life.

Look for the sights you enjoy seeing, and listen for sounds you enjoy hearing.

If it feels better to soften your gaze, do so. (See the Soft Gaze Walk on page 191.)

If you are feeling tense, you may wish to think of or envision yourself encased in a very thin layer of ice; and as you walk, the ice is melting, and you are feeling warmer, looser, less tense, more free in your breathing, and more capable in your steps.

Move your arms as you walk; and take moments when you stretch them wide open, allowing in life.

You may wish to count steps, knowing that each step connects you to the present, while also bringing you forward in life.

Feel free to sit or pause or even lie down if need be.

Also feel free to increase your pace, feel invigorated, and get a sweat going.

Every now and then, check in with your breath, and ask yourself, "How am I breathing?"

When an emotion or feeling comes up, be with it, rather than pushing it down. A good practice is to name it: "This is sadness," "This is anger," "This is fear," "This is clarity," "This is peace."

Then let it drift off, or run its course, as you continue to walk.

If you need to shout, yell, scream (or scream under your breath), and the location allows for it, do so. Conversely, if you feel the need or desire to laugh, sing, chant, pray, or recall a memory (or memories) aloud, or to express gratitude for all you experienced with someone or something you are now grieving over, do so.

Always allow yourself to take a few deep inhales and a few long, strong exhales—exhaling everything out that is ready to be released.

Go a distance that feels right, pushing yourself just enough to feel good, but not wear you out.

When you complete your walk, once again thank yourself for taking steps toward your healing.

TAKEAWAYS AND REFLECTIONS

Take your time as you reflect on your Grieving Walk and know that new freedoms, understandings, and pathways back to restored or increased well-being are being brought to the surface as you walk.

Grieving is a process and it is unique to each individual. When grieving, we must trust the process. Remember, just as Lao Tzu tells us, that "A journey of a thousand miles begins with a first step," so does the healing journey. I send you heartfelt love and the support of a thousand shining suns as you move through this trying time.

WALK 32
Working and Walking Things Out Walk

When we hear the other person's feelings and needs, we recognize our common humanity.

—MARSHALL B. ROSENBERG

OVERVIEW

"Clear the air." "Come to terms." "Make peace."

These are just three of the sayings that come to my mind when I think about the benefit that walking has when we need to work something out within ourselves or between ourselves and others.

The Working and Walking Things Out Walk is about heading off, releasing, diffusing (or transforming) highly charged or potentially charged situations; helping to break through and reinspire stalled talks and creative impasses; finding middle ground; growing mutual understanding; increasing communication; and opening to new, and often broader, perspectives.

> *It is often very helpful to remove ourselves from the charged space or room—and the history, and at times, distractions, that resides there—and head out for a walk or meet up for a walk on a more neutral or less charged ground to work and walk things out.*

When we feel challenged, scared, angry, depleted, "fixed in our ways," unsure, or overly certain that we are right, we tend to lock up, shut down, constrict, and become mentally and emotionally unmovable. *This* is the time for walking.

Walking shifts our mindset, opens us up, increases creativity, brings us more oxygen, relaxes us, and allows us to "move" into a sense of personal and interpersonal well-being that leads to resolution, inspiration, and deeper understanding.

Whether it be between family, friends, partners, ex-partners, soon-to-be ex-partners, co-workers, associates, neighbors, or lovers, or just one individual trying to work something out, the Working and Walking Things Out Walk is a highly effective way for getting back in sync and reaching common ground, or reaching a place of better understanding.

BENEFITS

- Helps resolve interpersonal conflicts.

- Walking beside others tends to naturally connect us in a deeper way. (Synchronistic movement helps bring synchronistic minds.)

- Frees you from familiar, or presently charged, environments, and the habits and patterns that reside there.

- Grows perspective and opens you up to creative solutions and inspired ideas.

- Allows you to *move* into resolution or deeper understanding.

- Promotes forward progress.

- Encourages you to breathe, feel, and open.

- Although eye contact is one of the cornerstones of effective communication, it is also not always comfortable. Walking beside one another allows us to pick our moments, and communicate in a way that feels best suited and most natural.

WHEN TO DO

- When needing to stave off a potential argument or resolve an ongoing issue or conflict in a more neutral, nurturing, or natural setting.

- When needing to work something out.

- When forward momentum is needed.

- When you're ready to, or need to, *move* toward a resolution or better understanding.

- When seeking greater clarity.

- When needing to open to the creativity, inspiration, and insight that walking brings.

HOW TO DO

Decide between yourselves that a Working and Walking Things Out Walk is something you and the concerned party or parties wish to do. Granted, there can be times when one person is more persuasive, and may know that engaging in this walk is the best option. If you are that person, use your powers of persuasion in the most positive and "best for all those involved" way. In other words, don't manipulate or force matters.

While it may be ideal to find a quiet, inspiring location that lends itself to a harmonious exchange, this may not be possible at the moment. So ... just *walk*.

And before you walk, use the restroom. Patience and presence are key when wanting to work and walk something out, but being patient and present while dealing with a full bladder is not always easy.

Hydrate. Avoid putting yourself into a position where you are suddenly thirsty and can't properly express yourself. Remember, when we are stressed, we *need* water. Hydration also helps all systems of the body to operate more smoothly, so drink.

The GBS Pre-Walk Check-In can certainly be helpful here. However, it could also be the last thing you want to do in this moment. So at the very least, *feel your feet on the ground* and *breathe*. If possible in the moment, or in moments during the walk, breathe along with your partner(s).

Set an intention. If you are in the state of mind, or can get yourself into the state of mind, to set an intention prior to starting off on the walk, do so. For example, "I/we will get through this with greater understanding" or "During this walk, I/we invite in peace and greater understanding." Throughout your walk, remember your intention. And if you alone or you and others are aligned with prayer, speak a prayer prior to walking, asking for the best outcome for all parties involved.

Out of respect for one another and the process, consider turning off your cellphone or switching it to airplane mode. If for some reason this is not something you feel comfortable with at this specific time, do your best not to check or respond to messages or prompts while walking.

Shake it off. Before you begin your walk, or perhaps at times during your walk, it may be helpful to take a moment to shake out your arms and legs. This will not only assist in releasing any bound-up tension you may be experiencing, but it will also open you up. You can even do it as a pair or a group. The sight of this alone may add levity and lighten the situation for you.

Relax your jaw, shoulders, and hands. (Don't worry, relaxing does not make you weak.)

At the onset of your walk, you may wish to place your hands palms-together against your heart center. Many people find this to be immediately calming and centering.

As you walk, there is no need to rush into words. You may even decide that it will serve each of you best to begin the walk in silence. (Not a passive-aggressive, stubborn silence, but a silence aligned with getting calmer, clearer, and more receptive.)

Respect the other's walking pace. Again, try to allow yourself to get more in sync, even if it's just for this walk.

During your communication, as best you can, concentrate on the positive and what is working, and on finding common ground. This is a great place to build and grow from.

Also, it's important to let the walk unfold—allow for spontaneity, inspiration, new direction, and answers to arrive from unseen places.

Collect your thoughts. Breathe. Don't make yourself small, and don't overinflate yourself.

Open to spaciousness. Take in the environment.

Allow yourself to see, hear, and experience the other person(s) as you walk, with an eye and ear toward greater understanding.

Also know that you may be planting seeds of change during this walk, and watering them in subsequent walks; so don't think you have to solve or understand everything in this moment.

Be on the lookout for the need to criticize, condemn, put down, or belittle your walking partner(s) or yourself. None of these tendencies will lead to the outcome and continued relational success you seek.

When things appear to be going off the rails, and the focus is straying from your intent, feel your feet on the ground, remain in control of (or connected to) your energies, and return to your breath.

If you find that things are getting too "heady" or you're losing your center, try to implement soft eyes (see the Soft Gaze Walk, page 191) and/or connecting deeper into your center (see the Centering Walk, page 165).

If things get too heated, breathe, return to your intent, and, if need be, agree to disagree, or suspend the walk.

Be respectful in your communication. Do your best not to blame or shame. Also respect the silence of the other. They could be deeply listening, feeling, processing, or just needing to be quiet within before speaking again.

Lastly, realize that we all look at, see, and process things in our own way. Allow room within yourself to view things from a new perspective, and also to be okay with the fact that change and new understandings—which at times can happen quickly—more often than not, take time.

Remember, this walk is about moving forward, advancing, opening—all toward a more positive outcome.

At the conclusion, honor yourself and those who walked with you for the willingness and desire to take healthy, productive steps.

Additional Practices You May Wish to Implement

If in the past there have been issues with interrupting or talking over one another, consider using a *talking stick*. The talking stick is used in various Native American traditions and is a great way to allow someone to speak and to be heard. Whoever is holding the stick in the moment talks. The rule is that the other person(s) does not interrupt. The stick can also be held in silence.

It does not have to be an actual talking stick (which you can purchase) or even a stick. It can be a coin, a feather, or any other comfortable-to-hold, neutral object. The main thing is to receive the words of the one holding it, as they will receive your words when you are holding it.

Another consideration is to burn sage prior to your walk. For those unfamiliar, variations of the herb sage have been used by indigenous peoples for centuries. It is often a ceremonial or pre-ceremonial practice to cleanse or purify a space (or individual) of any negativity. This may fall outside the realm of your belief system, but personally I've found that "smudging" (using sage to clear an area or person) is a highly beneficial way to help release the old, heavy, dense energies that surround us, and invite in the new. Smudging also generates negative ions, which, among other benefits (as discussed in the Rain Walk, page 74), helps to reduce stress.

TAKEAWAYS AND REFLECTIONS

It is my hope that the Working and Walking Things Out Walk brought you, at the very least, one step closer to the resolution, understanding, or outcome you seek. Whether alone or as a combined reflection, jot down, discuss, or make mental notes of all that was gained from your walk, and perhaps where you would still like to see improvements.

Commit to continuing to build upon what was shared, discovered, and hopefully healed or resolved, during your Working and Walking Things Out Walk. And continue on your own path of personal growth and self-discovery, always knowing that you are the one person that you can truly come to understand.

For additional helpful tools on communication and conflict resolution, I recommend looking into Nonviolent Communication techniques at www.nonviolentcommunication.com.

WALK 33
Head, Heart, Hara Walk

There is a vitality, a life force, an energy, a quickening,
that is translated through you into action, and because
there is only one of you in all time, this expression is
unique.

—MARTHA GRAHAM

OVERVIEW

The head. The heart. The hara. The three power centers of the body. Each of them unique but each connected to your overall makeup and contributing to your overall well-being.

To understand what makes them power centers, we'll take a look at them each individually and then explore them collectively.

The Head

The head needs no introduction. It houses the brain; this alone merits a standing ovation. It is the place within the human body that we most identify as the "place for answers." Rarely does one say, "Let me think about it," and then shift their focus to their heart or hara (although they may after this walk).

No, for better or for worse, the head is the long-established captain of the ship. It has earned that title through all it has bestowed upon us. But it is now time, even science is telling us so, to grow our understanding of, and connection to, other capable areas, and give the often overly taxed, overly relied-upon head some help.

The Heart

One would be hard-pressed to find a spiritual teaching that does not include the mystical properties of the heart. It has been referred to as the gateway to wisdom. The seat of compassion. The anchor of love. The home of the true self. I find it to be mysterious, wise, sensitive, and like the gut, very informative.

Just as scientists are now paying more attention to the gut-brain connection, there is also growing study into the heart-brain connection, and the uncharted (by science) territories—and deeper mysteries—of the heart. The HeartMath Institute is one such place that is dedicated to the greater understanding of an area of the human body that has inspired endless volumes of poetry, profound mystical teachings, and the gentleness of a dove.

Many of us have been taught that the brain is the only control center in the body, sending out signals that tell the heart what to do. But the institute has found that the heart also sends signals to the brain, perhaps sending even more signals than it receives. The heart influences emotional and cognitive functioning, just as the brain does. These two parts of the body work together.

When people dismiss the heart, saying things like "The heart is wicked" or "The heart is deceitful," they speak not of the heart but of the ego being projected onto the heart. The purity of the heart and heart center (the area in the center of your chest) does not house wickedness nor deceit nor jealousy, anger, or envy, unless *we* invite it in.

The Hara

We discussed the hara—also known as the "center"—quite a bit in the Centering Walk (page 165). We learned that the word originated in Japan; and although it refers to the center (or center of gravity within the human body), it also is considered a location within the body that stores great amounts of energy, or qi. So much so that the area—found two inches, or three finger-widths, below the navel in the center of the abdomen—is often referred to as the "sea of qi." It is a place of strength and power, often of mystical proportions, within the martial arts world. When your attention is dropped down into your hara, you feel rooted, stable, and strong, yet also buoyant.

The hara is also aligned with what has been called the body's second brain, or the "enteric brain" (since it is part of the enteric nervous system, a nervous system that works independently of the spine and brain) found in the gut. Science continues to study this enteric brain for the gut-brain connection, giving us greater insight into everything from how we process information within the gut, to how we process foods, to how we experience that often-unexplainable "gut feeling" or "gut knowing," and how the gut can affect even our mental well-being.

The "Head, Heart, Hara Walk" connects us deeply into the places where we feel the most, hear the most, sense the most, intuit the most, and at times, ignore the most.

It is yet another unique way in which to expand awareness, increase vitality, and reduce stress.

BENEFITS

- Helps you to connect deeper into three of the main feeling and decision-making areas of the body.

- Allows you to see how each of the three areas provides something unique to your overall makeup and well-being.

- Allows you to experience holding thoughts and questions in each of the three areas.

- Grows your overall mind-body awareness, and opens you to new ways of processing and receiving information.

- Helps you to understand that not all answers, insights, and direction are born of the mind.

WHEN TO DO

- When you want to tap into the information, feelings, and power of these three unique centers.

- When you wish to seek or source answers, insights, and direction from different centers of the body.

- When ready to grow your awareness to value the heart and hara as capable and profound guiding systems.

- When wisdom, feeling, and sensing beyond the reach of the head are sought.

- When wanting to experience moving your focused attention (and connection) between these three centers of the body.

HOW TO DO

Performing this walk with a partner who can talk and walk you through the instructions can be helpful.

Select the area in which you'd like to walk. Consider a space that has limited distractions.

Turn off your cellphone, switch it to airplane mode, or leave it behind.

Perform your GBS Pre-Walk Check-In.

Begin to walk in a regular, mindful manner: aware of the ground beneath you, the breath within you (including cycles of inhalation and exhalation), and the space around you.

After you settle into a rhythm, you will start to tune into each of the three focus areas: the head, the heart center, and the hara.

As you walk, begin by identifying each of these areas with a light touch or tap.

Touch around the different parts of your head, then the heart, and then the hara.

Now that you've made a physical connection, use your imagination, sensing, or simply your "placed attention" to connect you one at a time into each of these areas.

As you continue to walk, focus on the space within your head; this includes the brain. Allow your attention and focus to remain there as you walk for a minute or more.

Then shift your focus and attention to the heart center and the heart itself. Allow your attention and focus to remain there as you walk for a minute or more.

Then shift your focus and attention to your hara. Allow your attention and focus to remain there as you walk for a minute or more.

For each of these three areas, allow your concentration to fill the area and your breathing to just remain natural.

Next ...

As you walk, shift the focus of your breath so that you are inhaling into your head. Focus on breathing and drawing oxygen into your head, filling your brain and all the space around it. Do this five or six times. (Hold each breath in this location for three or more seconds.)

Then breathe into your heart center and your heart itself, filling it with breath. Do this five or six times. (Hold each breath in this location for three or more seconds.)

Then breathe into your hara, filling your lower abdomen and your center with breath. Do this five or six times. (Hold each breath in this location for three or more seconds.)

Next ...

Now go through the same progression—head, heart, hara—but this time you are going to envision white light filling each of the areas.

First envision your head and the space around your head filled with a beautiful white light. Walk like this for a minute or so.

Then envision your heart center filled with a beautiful white light. Walk like this for a minute or so.

Then envision your hara filled with a beautiful white light. Walk like this for a minute or so.

Then alternate between each of them: put your focus and light in your head for a few seconds, then your heart, then your hara, then repeat. You can switch up and vary the order in any way you'd like, including what you may intuitively feel to do.

Next ...

Take a thought and hold it first in your head. Just continue walking, seeing what may arise or what it becomes.

Then place the same thought in your heart center. Continue walking, seeing what may arise or what it becomes.

Then place that same thought in your hara. Continue walking, seeing what may arise or what it becomes.

Next ...

Consider a problem or question you may have.

Hold it first in your head. Just continue walking, seeing what may arise.

Then place that same problem in your heart center. Continue walking, seeing what may arise.

Then place that same problem in your hara. Continue walking, seeing what may arise.

Repeat this for any number of thoughts, problems, or questions, always allowing for things (answers, insights, inspiration, and even uncertainty) to arise naturally, with you never trying to force anything.

Conclude your walk by once again breathing into each of the three areas.

Then touching each of the areas.

Then thanking each of the areas.

End in gratitude.

TAKEAWAYS AND REFLECTIONS

What was the Head, Heart, Hara Walk like for you? Did you find yourself naturally connecting into one of the three areas easier than the other areas?

What did it feel like focusing light in each area? Was one area easier to envision bathed in light than another?

Did your thoughts, problems, and questions take on a different feel, form, or even answer, when you placed them in the different areas?

Jot down or make mental notes of any takeaways and reflections you may have. And work with these three areas whenever you feel the need or desire to view (and process) things from different areas and aspects of your body.

WALK 34
Seeing from Different Parts of Your Body Walk

Genius, in truth, is little more than the faculty of perceiving in an unhabitual way.

—WILLIAM JAMES

OVERVIEW

Picture an eye in your shoulder. Picture an eye in your hip. Picture an eye in your heart. Or even your big toe.

Of all the walks in this book, this one may strike you as the oddest—or most unique. It was born of an exercise that my Awareness Through Movement teacher occasionally has us do, where we pretend to have an eye in different parts of our body and then view the rest of our body—and the space around us—from this position in the body. We do this while lying on the floor.

Having felt the awareness-building, brain-stimulating value of the exercise, I decided to try it while walking. It has since become one of the most informative, and also challenging, walks for me and others I walk with.

The majority of us are just beginning to explore what it means to live and move in our human body. We are just now learning about the depth of the mind-body connection, brain neuroplasticity, sensing, the human energy field, the quantifiable benefits of meditation, and who we are as spiritual beings. These are exciting times.

As many of you discovered while performing the Centering Walk (page 165), it feels different when you shift focus from seeing everything from behind your eyes to seeing or, in the case of the Centering Walk, focusing/moving from your center.

The Seeing from Different Parts of Your Body Walk will bring you deep into the present, and awaken in you a greater sense and ability to tune into your body, and its unlived in or unrecognized places, and then tune into the world from these places.

Just as the Inner Smile Walk (page 82) allowed you to connect to and bring warmth into specific parts of your body while walking, the Seeing from Different Parts of Your Body Walk will allow you to (and teach you how to) focus both inwardly and outwardly, and in a sense "see" from, and with, various parts of your body.

Even though I use the word "parts" in the title and throughout this walk/exercise, we often come to realize, at times through walks like this, that there are no separate *parts,* and everything is interrelated, even though we experience, and most often treat, the body as if its parts are separate.

Will this walk give you superpowers? Maybe.

BENEFITS

- Connects you to your body in new, interesting, and enlivening ways.
- Allows you to develop a larger awareness of how you focus, sense, and see.
- Opens you to a greater curiosity and creativity.
- Allows you to better sense, feel, and experience the interconnected, holistic nature of yourself.
- Anchors you deeper into your body.
- Stimulates your brain.
- Helps you to better recognize and connect into the unlived in or unrecognized areas of your body.
- Brings you into the present.

WHEN TO DO

- When wanting to connect deeper into your body and to grow the mind-body connection.
- When wanting to explore the interconnected nature of self.
- When needing to, or wanting to, open up and expand the way you see and experience the world.

- When wanting to grow your creativity and your appreciation for how you move through life.
- When wanting to experience a very interesting way of walking.
- When wanting to stimulate your brain.

NOTE Since this exercise engages the brain in a way that many people are not used to, this walk can at times be tiring. Consider it a mental workout, and be gentle with yourself.

HOW TO DO

As I shared earlier, this exercise was introduced to me as a floor exercise to be done while lying down in a relaxed position with the choice of having the eyes open or closed. This may be something you'd like to try prior to performing the exercise while walking. Or you can step right into it.

Doing this walk with a partner who can guide you through the instructions can be helpful.

Whether walking alone, with a partner, or as a group, choose your location.

Turn off your cellphone, switch it to airplane mode, or leave it behind.

An affirmation or intention for this walk can be: "I see and experience myself, my body, and the world around me in new and interesting ways."

There are in essence three parts to this walk: the preparation; viewing the inner and outer body from your placed eye; then viewing the outer world from the placed eye.

Also, even though this may require a different type of focus and "placed attention" than you are used to, keep it fun. Frustration tends to limit your vision, no matter what type of seeing you're engaged in.

Perform your GBS Pre-Walk Check-In.

Begin walking.

As you walk, take in your surroundings as you normally would, through your eyes (of course allowing for all the other senses as well).

Continue to walk mindfully, feeling and hearing the movement of your body and your feet on the ground.

As you continue, practice your soft gaze (see the Soft Gaze Walk, page 191), allowing your eyes to soften and relax, your field of vision (including peripheral vision) to expand to its fullness, and the hard edges of the world to soften.

Breathe fully and deeply, inhaling through the nose and exhaling through the mouth, and walk like this for a few minutes, allowing yourself to become as relaxed and present as possible.

You are now going to begin the exercise of seeing from different parts of your body.

When you do so, you will of course still have your normal vision to rely upon (although there will be times when I suggest you close your eyes), but allow yourself to go as deeply into the exercise as you can.

You will find that your regular eyes are going to want to move in the direction you are thinking about and setting your focus on with your placed eye. This is fine, and natural. Over time, you can reduce the extent of this. Using soft eyes, and taking moments to close your eyes, assists in doing so.

Once you have established the area and placed the eye there (and the eye can be any shape, size, or color that you'd like), you will begin to see from that area.

Because of the nature of how deeply into your system this walk works, we will only work/play from one area the first time performing this exercise.

How to Do: From the Heart Center to the Self

In general, you can begin anywhere in the body that you'd like, but I will begin the instructions with the heart. At the end of the How to Do section, I will go into more detail on how to do this exercise from multiple parts of your body and will encourage you to move the eye through different areas of the body.

As you walk, envision an eye either in your heart itself, or in your heart center location at the center of your chest.

You will now see/view the rest of your body—and later the world outside of you—first and foremost from your heart. Unlike your regular eyes, this placed eye has no limitations; it can look in any direction, including behind you.

At first, it may help to pause your walk at times to tune deeper into the exercise.

With your regular eyes looking forward, let your "placed eye" look throughout your body.

It may feel very strange at first—a cross between "What the heck am I doing?" and "This hurts my head." Don't force it.

Allow the placed eye to focus anywhere you would like it to, and also form connections via creating sight lines, connecting this area of the body (the heart) to other areas within you.

For example, look from your heart to your hip, and make a connection with a line (you can even imagine the line lit up). Look up to the head, the shoulders, then down to the pelvis, knees, and feet, then look at your back, and the length of your spine from your heart.

Remember, you can pause with your eyes closed at times, especially when you need extra help tuning into an area.

How to Do: From the Heart Center to the Outer World

Having explored the inside and outside of your body from your placed eye, now look from the heart center (or wherever you chose to place the eye) to the *outer world*, viewing everything in your regular field of vision, and beyond—including the space behind you—from your placed eye.

Really try to see from this area. In the same way you made a sight-line connection within your body, now envision a line connection from your heart to whatever it is your heart's eye is looking at.

You may go one step further by asking yourself—in whatever body part you are currently aligned with—how would this part of me perceive the world? What is my shoulder's view of the world? What does my hand say about the world? And in this case, what does my heart say and feel about the world?

You will conclude your walk by settling back into your normal vision and continuing walking for any distance you'd like, while also still feeling into the connections made.

How to Do: From Multiple Parts of Your Body

Remember, this exercise can be mentally tiring. Since we want to use this walk to become more alive, more vital, it's best not to overexert yourself by taking on too much.

Just as you began with the heart, you will choose your initial starting point—this may be an instinctual, intuitive, or random choice, or simply a *fun* choice.

Go through the original steps/instructions: breathing, feeling your connection to the ground, applying a soft gaze (relaxed eyes), and generally relaxing yourself.

Begin from your chosen starting/seeing position, look in any and all directions within the body or along the outside of the body, and make connections from place to place by envisioning a line form between the places. Feel each area come alive—or light up from your attention (and stay lit as you then move the imaginary eye to the next area)—then shift your focus to seeing/connecting to areas outside the body, in your environment.

You can continue to work/play in this manner as you move your "placed eye" from area to area.

You may wish to physically pause prior to moving the imaginary eye to its next area, or you may wish to do so while in stride. Be as creative and inspired as you can; you can envision the eye at the end of your toe, or at your fingertip (pointing your finger in any direction and seeing out of it), or in any joint within your body.

TAKEAWAYS AND REFLECTIONS

What was the Seeing from Different Parts of Your Body Walk like for you?

Were you able to place your attention into specific areas and then see or "sense" from those areas?

Did you feel it required, and offered, a new form of focus or awareness?

Could you feel the area light up as you placed your attention there?

Did anything surprise you about the walk?

Jot down or make mental notes of any takeaways and reflections you may have, and anticipate that this walk will continue to work on you long after it's completed.

Whether while walking, seated, or lying down, continue to tune into this exercise, stimulating your brain and deepening your mind-body, mind-world connection.

WALK 35
Childlike Wonder Walk

He who can no longer pause to wonder and stand rapt in awe is as good as dead; his eyes are closed.

—ALBERT EINSTEIN

OVERVIEW

Perhaps he is not as good as dead, as Einstein stated, but he is certainly asleep to a great deal of life.

During the process of writing this book, I came across two videos that had gone viral. One was of a man who was born colorblind and was given special glasses to see color. The other was of a woman born deaf who received a cochlear implant and could now hear for the first time in her life.

As you can imagine, they could barely contain themselves. Their excitement and raw emotion took hold of them in such a way that viewers were moved to the depth of their being. These stories speak so deeply to what many of us take for granted, and yet are one more reason for me to share this walk.

To varying degrees, the large majority of us have all our senses intact and can see and hear across a wide spectrum.

There are many reasons why we shut down our sense of awe and wonder. Some of it comes from "growing up," "becoming an adult," learning to "live in the real world," and of course "having seen it all and figured it all out." And some of it is just that many people, perhaps yourself included, have lived a challenging life, where magic, awe, and wonder may have been stripped away.

Also factor in that most of us are moving at the speed of modern life, which generally does not lend itself to enchantment, curiosity, and wonder.

The good news is that your sense of wonder can be reclaimed, and the innocent, wonder-filled view of a child can once again be experienced as an adult. You can retrain yourself to be curious and perhaps see everything as a miracle, including yourself. When you walk present and mindfully, you can invite these qualities back in.

The Childlike Wonder Walk is a step back in time, to the wonder and curiosity that once ran your entire life. It's an invitation to see and hear the world with eyes and ears anew—while engaging all your other senses.

BENEFITS

- Reawakens a sense of curiosity, wonder, and awe.
- Connects you to the child within.
- Elevates your appreciation of life and helps you to see everyday things anew.
- Reconnects you to a time of innocence.
- Opens you to larger perspectives and creative inspiration.
- Helps you to *feel*.
- Elevates your mood.
- Brings you into the present and enriches your day-to-day, moment-to-moment experience.
- Bonds you with your child, children in general, and that place of innocence within.

WHEN TO DO

- When you seek to reconnect to the wonder and awe of the world we live in.
- When needing to regain a sense of innocence and reopen yourself to the way you once saw and experienced life.
- When no longer wanting to be cynical, or too serious.
- When wanting to slow down, become fully present, and reengage the child within.

- When wanting to be like Einstein.
- When wanting to feel better.
- Perform the Childlike Wonder Walk alone or with a child to guide you.

HOW TO DO

Choose a time and place that will allow for you to activate your curiosity, reclaim a sense of innocence, and get lost in wonder. As the purpose of this walk is to look for the wonder in everyday life, you do not need to choose a special place already packed with magic, like Disneyland or a butterfly sanctuary, unless you truly wish to do so.

Some affirmations to consider: "I allow childlike wonder to guide me." "With all the senses of my being, I fully experience the world." "I invite in awe and wonder." "I experience the world anew."

Turn off your cellphone, switch it to airplane mode, or leave it behind.

Whether it be on your own, or with a partner, group, or family member, perform your GBS Pre-Walk Check-In.

Begin walking.

Start slow, and remain slow—unless you want to at times experience the wonder of moving quickly. Feel free to pause, and as Einstein shared, "stand rapt in awe."

Simply put, during your Childlike Wonder Walk, you will look at everything, including the fine hairs on your arm, as if it's your first time seeing it: viewing, hearing, touching, feeling, and smelling the world as if you were a captivated explorer from a distant planet.

Embrace curiosity and enchantment.

Allow your "feeling body" to be activated, and allow yourself to be moved.

See what you are naturally drawn to.

If walking with a child or children, rather than taking pictures of the child seeing or experiencing something for the first time, put your cellphone away and experience it with them. Follow their eyes, where they point, what they gesture toward, what they ask questions about, what they are listening to, what they stare at in awe with no proper means of explaining what is before their eyes.

Allow for any captivating or awe-inspiring memories from your childhood to return.

Feel free to reexperience or even reenact any special moment that flashes into you, now that you are open to it.

While you're at it, see if you can pinpoint the time when the world no longer held you spellbound.

A child does not have any intellectual understanding of a god or science, or a combination of both; the child is simply with what is before them. Be the child.

Look for the interconnectedness of nature, and everything else.

Allow yourself to turn 360 degrees while saying the simple word "Wow."

Allow joy and laughter to emerge.

Breathe into moments of wonder, reminding yourself, "I am alive, and I am fortunate to experience this."

Continue your walk for as long as you'd like, and continue to allow the wonders of the world to reach into you. As you do, place within you this quote by Papiha Ghosh: "In my soul, I am still that small child who did not care about anything else but the beautiful colors of a rainbow."

TAKEAWAYS AND REFLECTIONS

What did you learn from your Childlike Wonder Walk? Could you return to the innocence and curiosity that once resided within you? Did it feel odd to slow yourself way down and really explore and experience the world around you?

Can you see how this walk can carry over into your everyday life, growing and enriching your earthly experience?

Jot down or make mental notes of any takeaways and reflections you may have. And continue to allow yourself—and the curious child within—to experience the miracle that is life.

Conclusion

AS WE HAVE EXPLORED throughout this book, awareness is key to greater overall well-being, and walking is a tremendous way to bring us into heightened awareness. The trick now is to carry these principles beyond your allotted walk time and make them an ever-increasing part of your life. As you do, you will grow in greater self-understanding, self-realization, and ultimately, if so desired, self-mastery.

I invite you to allow the world—both inner and outer—to open and communicate with you in new, exciting, and deeply revealing ways.

But most of all, have fun, and allow joy into your life. Welcome ease as a friend, and a powerful one at that. Remember, nothing in this book has to be done perfectly. We're all a work in progress—and wonderful works in progress at that.

Remember your GBS, and thanks again for walking with me.

May your walks awaken you, and may *your* walk awaken others.

Blessings on your path.

Glenn

"Which Walk to Do When" Guide

THE FOLLOWING WILL ASSIST YOU in selecting which of the thirty-five walks may be most beneficial for you based on your current physical, mental, emotional, or spiritual needs.

Each of these walks can be implemented for groups, families, and children, but you will also find specific suggestions for each of these categories at the conclusion of this reference guide.

When feeling anxious or overwhelmed

Centering Walk	165
Barefoot Grounding Walk	70
Soft Gaze Walk	191
Inner Smile Walk	82
Walking Meditation (There and Back Style)	99
Gratitude Walk	151
Water Walk	78
Prayer Walk	140

When feeling angry

Slow-Fast Walk	178
Seeing Walk	158
Centering Walk	165
Working and Walking Things Out Walk	205
Walking Meditation (Walking the Labyrinth)	108
Head, Heart, Hara Walk	211
Barefoot Grounding Walk	70
Gratitude Walk	151

When feeling sluggish or low energy

Slow-Fast Walk	178
Barefoot Grounding Walk	70
Centering Walk	165

When feeling bored

Making the World (or at Least Your Neighborhood) a Cleaner Place Walk	95
Water Walk	78
Earth Below, Heavens Above Walk	116
Backward Walk	195
Slow Motion Walk	186
Heel to Toe and Toe to Heel Balance Walks	53
Seeing from Different Parts of Your Body Walk	217
Listening Walk	89

When traveling

Listening Walk	89
Seeing Walk	158
Outer Smile Walk	85
Barefoot Grounding Walk	70
Gratitude Walk	151
Childlike Wonder Walk	224

When sad

Gratitude Walk	151
Outer Smile Walk	85
Inner Smile Walk	82
Grieving Walk	200
Childlike Wonder Walk	224
Affirmation Walk	145
Dedication Walk	137
Prayer Walk	140
Slow-Fast Walk	178
Walking Meditation (There and Back Style)	99

When preparing for a meeting or presentation

Walking Meditation (There and Back Style)	99
Walking Meditation (Circle Style)	104
Centering Walk	165
Slow-Fast Walk	178
Destination-Manifestation Walk	112

When wanting to explore and increase inner and outer balance and stability

Heel to Toe and Toe to Heel Balance Walks	53
Turning and Tilting Your Head Balance Walk	61
Centering Walk	165
Slow Motion Walk	186
Backward Walk	195

When needing the world to slow down

Slow Motion Walk	186
Walking Meditation (There and Back Style)	99
Walking Meditation (Circle Style)	104
Walking Meditation (Walking the Labyrinth)	108
Soft Gaze Walk	191
Barefoot Grounding Walk	70
Water Walk	78
Childlike Wonder Walk	224

When needing to become more present

Walking Awake through Your Living Space	65
Seeing Walk	158
Listening Walk	89
Barefoot Grounding Walk	70
Walking Meditation (There and Back Style)	99
Walking Meditation (Circle Style)	104
Walking Meditation (Walking the Labyrinth)	108
Seeing from Different Parts of Your Body Walk	217
Mindfully Walking Your Dog Walk	124

When wanting to stimulate creativity or expand perspective

Soft Gaze Walk	191
Head, Heart, Hara Walk	211
Seeing Walk	158
Walking Awake through Your Living Space	65
Seeing from Different Parts of Your Body Walk	217
Walking Meditation (Walking the Labyrinth)	108

When wanting to manifest something into your life

Affirmation Walk	145
Destination-Manifestation Walk	112
Prayer Walk	140

When wanting to feel closer to the divine or your own indwelling spirit

Earth Below, Heavens Above Walk	116
Prayer Walk	140
Gratitude Walk	151
Full Moon Walk	120
Childlike Wonder Walk	224
Walking Meditation (Circle Style)	104
Walking Meditation (Walking the Labyrinth)	108

When grieving the loss of someone or something

Grieving Walk	200
Dedication Walk	137
Water Walk	78
Earth Below, Heavens Above Walk	116

When needing to feel more at peace

Walking Meditation (There and Back Style)	99
Walking Meditation (Circle Style)	104
Walking Meditation (Walking the Labyrinth)	108
Water Walk	78
Inner Smile Walk	82

When needing to feel more at peace *(continued)*

Earth Below, Heavens Above Walk 116

Soft Gaze Walk 191

Barefoot Grounding Walk 70

Prayer Walk 140

When needing to boost your confidence

Affirmation Walk 145

Destination-Manifestation Walk 112

Inner Smile Walk 82

Gratitude Walk 151

Centering Walk 165

When needing to forgive yourself or others

Forgiving Yourself Walk 133

Forgiving Others Walk 129

Working and Walking Things Out Walk 205

When needing answers

Head, Heart, Hara Walk 211

Listening Walk 89

Barefoot Grounding Walk 70

Earth Below, Heavens Above Walk 116

Water Walk 78

Prayer Walk 140

When needing to escape from the world, or at least your thoughts

Earth Below, Heavens Above Walk 116

Water Walk 78

Listening Walk 89

When needing a restorative break from screen time

Soft Gaze Walk 191

Barefoot Grounding Walk 70

Centering Walk 165

Water Walk 78

When needing to quiet your mind

Walking Meditation (There and Back Style)	99
Walking Meditation (Circle Style)	104
Slow Motion Walk	186
Heel to Toe and Toe to Heel Balance Walks	53
Centering Walk	165
Walking Meditation (Walking the Labyrinth)	108
Rain Walk	74
Water Walk	78
Barefoot Grounding Walk	70
Affirmation Walk	145

When in the midst of change and challenges

Centering Walk	165
Barefoot Grounding Walk	70
Head, Heart, Hara Walk	211
Gratitude Walk	151
Affirmation Walk	145
Prayer Walk	140
Walking Meditation (There and Back Style)	99
Walking Meditation (Walking the Labyrinth)	108
Working and Walking Things Out Walk	205

When wanting to grow bodily awareness and stimulate your brain

Backward Walk	195
Heel to Toe and Toe to Heel Balance Walks	53
Turning and Tilting Your Head Balance Walk	61
Slow Motion Walk	186
Seeing from Different Parts of Your Body Walk	217
Head, Heart, Hara Walk	211
Inner Smile Walk	82
Centering Walk	165

When wanting to increase focus

Walking Meditation (There and Back Style)	99
Walking Meditation (Circle Style)	104
Walking Meditation (Walking the Labyrinth)	108
Slow Motion Walk	186
Destination-Manifestation Walk	112
Heel to Toe and Toe to Heel Balance Walks	53
Listening Walk	89
Seeing Walk	158
Head, Heart, Hara Walk	211

When having moved to a new location

Walking Awake through Your Living Space	65
Seeing Walk	158
Listening Walk	89
Barefoot Grounding Walk	70

When in a city or other crowded location

Crowd Walking	172
Centering Walk	165

When in nature

Barefoot Grounding Walk	70
Seeing Walk	158
Listening Walk	89
Walking Meditation (There and Back Style)	104
Full Moon Walk	120
Earth Below, Heavens Above Walk	116
Rain Walk	74
Making the World (or at Least Your Neighborhood) a Cleaner Place Walk	95
Childlike Wonder Walk	224
Water Walk	78

When in nature *(continued)*

Soft Gaze Walk	191
Outer Smile Walk	85
Destination-Manifestation Walk	112

When restricted to indoor/in-home walking or just wanting to be inside

Heel to Toe and Toe to Heel Balance Walks	53
Walking Meditation (There and Back Style)	99
Centering Walk	165
Backward Walk	195
Slow Motion Walk	186
Walking Awake through Your Living Space	65

When walking on a treadmill

Slow-Fast Walk	178
Inner Smile Walk	82
Gratitude Walk	151
Affirmation Walk	145
Head, Heart, Hara Walk	211

For groups and families, trust-building, bonding, further discovery, or community-unifying

Seeing Walk	158
Listening Walk	89
Gratitude Walk	151
Making the World (or at Least Your Neighborhood) a Cleaner Place Walk	95
Full Moon Walk	120
Earth Below, Heavens Above Walk	116
Rain Walk	74
Centering Walk	165
Seeing from Different Parts of Your Body Walk	217
Slow Motion Walk	186
Backward Walk	195

For groups and families, trust-building, bonding, further discovery, or community-unifying *(continued)*

Heel to Toe and Toe to Heel Balance Walks	53
Turning and Tilting Your Head Balance Walk	61
Dedication Walk	137
Water Walk	78
Walking Meditation (Walking the Labyrinth)	108

For kids

Slow Motion Walk	186
Backward Walk	195
Seeing Walk	158
Listening Walk	89
Walking Awake through Your Living Space	65
Rain Walk	74
Earth Below, Heavens Above Walk	116
Centering Walk	165
Barefoot Grounding Walk	70
Gratitude Walk	151
Heel to Toe and Toe to Heel Balance Walks	53
Outer Smile Walk	85
Inner Smile Walk	82

Affirmations and Intentions for Walking

MANY OF THE WALKS in this collection offer examples of affirmations to practice while walking. Other walks suggest setting a mental intention prior to beginning your walk. These can be empowering tools to deepen your experience while engaging in the walks. What follows is a list of affirmations and intentions, along with the walks they correspond to.

Affirmations

WALK 1. HEEL TO TOE AND TOE
TO HEEL BALANCE WALKS

"My balance is getting better and better."

"In all areas of my life and being, my balance improves daily."

"My balance is perfect."

WALK 11. WALKING MEDITATION
(THERE AND BACK STYLE)

"As I walk, I am calm."

"With each step I feel calmer and more centered."

"I am here."

WALK 12. WALKING MEDITATION
(CIRCLE STYLE)

"As I walk this circle, I return to wholeness."

"In body, mind, and spirit, I am whole and complete."

"I walk this circle in complete trust."

WALK 13. WALKING MEDITATION
(WALKING THE LABYRINTH)

"Walking this labyrinth, I receive all I need to receive, and I release all I need to release."

"As I walk this labyrinth, I am open to receive my highest good."

"I walk this labyrinth for the highest good of all."

WALK 19. FORGIVING YOURSELF WALK

"I am loved, and I am love."

"I forgive myself."

WALK 22. AFFIRMATION WALK

"I allow time for my personal well-being."

"I will find a job."

"The job I need is heading my way. I take the right steps to meet it."

"I have a job."

"I am lovable."

"Life is beautiful."

"I openly accept love into all aspects of my life and being."

"I grow from life's challenges."

"I love myself."

"I am healthy."

"I am safe."

"I am valuable."

"Life works."

"Everything will be okay."

"The answers and insights I need arrive at the perfect time."

"I approve of myself."

"I get stronger every day."

"I look for and see the good in all people, including myself."

"It's okay to rest."

WALK 25. CENTERING WALK
(A.K.A. WALKING FROM YOUR CENTER)

"Stable, fluid, and balanced, I move from my center with ease."

WALK 26. CROWD WALKING

"I hold my ground and claim my space no matter the energies around me."

"I am safe."

"I flow with strength and ease."

WALK 31. GRIEVING WALK

"With each step I take, I find peace."

"I am safe."

WALK 34. SEEING FROM DIFFERENT
PARTS OF YOUR BODY WALK

"I see and experience myself, my body, and the world around me in new and interesting ways."

WALK 35. CHILDLIKE WONDER WALK

"I allow childlike wonder to guide me."

"With all the senses of my being, I fully experience the world."

"I invite in awe and wonder."

"I experience the world anew."

"I am alive, and I am fortunate to experience this."

Intentions

WALK 3. WALKING AWAKE
THROUGH YOUR LIVING SPACE

"I will now see, hear, feel, and sense anything in my living space that needs to be seen, heard, felt, or sensed for my highest good and the highest good of all."

WALK 6. WATER WALK

"I would like to let go of my past hurts."

"I will now allow inspiration to enter me."

"I will leave here more peaceful than when I arrived."

"I will no longer feel small."

"I will once again find my flow."

WALK 18. FORGIVING OTHERS WALK

"I walk this walk in forgiveness, now ready and willing to release what no longer serves me and my highest good."

WALK 19. FORGIVING YOURSELF WALK

"I walk this walk in forgiveness of myself; it is now time."

"Through this walk, I invite self-forgiveness into every fiber of my being."

WALK 23. GRATITUDE WALK

"With this walk, I will discover gratitude within and around me in ways that elevate my understanding of and appreciation for all life."

WALK 24. SEEING WALK

"I will now see all that is for my highest good and deepening awareness to see."

WALK 32. WORKING AND WALKING THINGS OUT WALK

"I/we will get through this with greater understanding."

"During this walk, I/we invite in peace and greater understanding."

WALK 34. SEEING FROM DIFFERENT PARTS OF YOUR BODY WALK

"I see and experience myself, my body, and the world around me in new and interesting ways."

Acknowledgments

THE LIST OF THOSE who contributed to my path, and therefore this book, is long and winds through many chapters of a life's journey that has been anything but conventional. I've been blessed first and foremost with a family who "got me," and always gave me room to be me. Within the wide breadth of this lived exploration, I have found that all roads truly lead back to the one—the interconnectedness of all. Therefore, I thank all.

With that said, to my friends, teachers, and guides (both seen and unseen), thank you for your prompts, whispers, and reflections, and for always showing up at the right time.

To the many humans who maintain our streets, roads, sidewalks, trails, and paths, thank you.

To those who walked with me when I had little to give, and to those who walked beside me when I had all of me to give, thank you.

To the artists, the explorers, and the great minds who have brought forth immense contributions born of solitary walks, thank you.

To my brother, Pete, for so strongly walking your path, while always supporting mine, thank you. To my mother, Elbjorg, a saint perhaps; if not, a friend I wish all could experience: thank you. Our walks, our talks, and our shared appreciations of life shall live on in me through eternity, and continue to nourish my knowing that there is far more good in this world than bad. To my late father, Rudolf, who was able to read the preface to this book and remind me that no one wants to know our dog's name. As with most things, he was probably right. But her name was Tanya, and he loved her as he loved us. As I write this, I hope he's walking beside her. I love you, Dad. Thank you for everything, including giving me an eye for detail.

Thank you to Mister Fred Rogers for being a calm presence reaching into the heart of a young boy through the magic of a Zenith TV, for making kindness cool, and for reminding us all that we're special. I would have loved to have walked through your neighborhood, or any neighborhood, with you.

Dennis Swenson, thank you for your continued encouragement, your friendship, and all you give to humanity, including facilitating hundreds of "walk and talk sessions" for those in need.

Randy Cherner, you are a teacher and healer extraordinaire. Thank you for bringing so many home to their true selves, and for making effortless effort real. This book would not be in the hands of others if not for you.

Navyo Ericsen, a gem and a brother, thank you for your presence, and for reading my words in whatever form I present them.

Sal Marotta, thank you for bringing your clarity, energy, and enthusiasm to my path and this walking book, and doing so from the "old neighborhood."

Carmine Del Sordi, Davis Alexander, Jeff Butler, Michael Wenrich, Ned Specktor, Cassie Jaye, and Andy Geller, you have always been there for me and my work. Thank you.

Isabelle Daikeler, thank you for a friendship forged in the stars.

Tristan Destry Saldaña, your depth of character and love of the written word are beyond inspiring. Thank you for pouring some of your brilliance into my cup.

Richard Grossinger and Lindy Hough, my deepest gratitude to you for starting North Atlantic Books and helping so many important works find their way into the world. Richard, thank you for writing some of my favorite books, including *Planet Medicine.*

Joel Friedlander, thank you for your friendship and all you do on behalf of authors.

Finally, to the team at North Atlantic Books, especially Shayna Keyles and Adrienne Armstrong—thank you for making this book better.

About the Author

GLENN BERKENKAMP has explored and shared ultimate wellness and inspired living through the mind-body-spirit connection for a quarter century. His talks, workshops, and writings elevate our daily experience, unite us in something greater, and bring us to a larger awareness of who we are. From this space, the impossible often becomes possible; the ordinary, beautiful; and the miraculous, our home. A former bodybuilder and fitness expert, Glenn is a story-teller, screenwriter, transformational speaker, walk leader, and creator of the Writing Into The Now workshop. He is the author of *Mastery: Living the Highest You* and *Would My Heart Think This Thought?* As a screenwriter, he has collaborated with Academy Award–winning producers and earned the respect of A-list actors. He resides in Northern California.

Connect with Glenn on the following platforms:

Website: LivingTheHighestYou.com

Facebook: @authorglennberkenkamp

Instagram: @glennberkenkamp